TO CARE FOR THE EARTH

TO CARE FOR THE EARTH

a call to a new theology

Sean McDonagh

BEAR & COMPANY
SANTA FE, NEW MEXICO

Library of Congress Cataloging-in-Publication Data

McDonagh, Sean, 1935-
  To care for the earth.

  Includes index.
  Bibliography: p. 215
  1. Nature—Religious aspects—Christianity.
2. Human ecology—Religious aspects—Christianity.
I. Title.
BT695.5.M43   1987   261.8'362   87-14507
ISBN 0-939680-42-4

First U.S. edition published in 1987 by
Bear & Company
P.O. Drawer 2860, Santa Fe, NM 87501

First published in 1986 by Cassell Ltd., England

Cover Photography: James R. Stewart
Cover Design: Angela C. Werneke
Printed in the United States of America by BookCrafters
10 9 8 7 6 5 4 3 2

CONTENTS

Part 2   A Call to a New Theology

ACKNOWLEDGEMENTS

The author and the publishers gratefully acknowledge permission to use material on which the following hold copyright:

Thames & Hudson Ltd for a poem taken from *Celtic Mysteries: The Ancient Religion* (1975) by John Sharkey.

New Writers' Press and Michael Hartnett for a poem entitled 'Marban, a hermit speaks' (1974) by Michael Hartnett.

Franciscan Herald Press for the poem entitled 'The Canticle of Brother Sun' by St Francis of Assisi, Omnibus Source.

Bear & Co. Inc. for an extract taken from *Meditations with Hildegarde of Bingen* by Hildegarde of Bingen.

FOREWORD

Watching a TV film one night on the predicted effects of 'nuclear winter', I was joined by my young nephew. Suspecting that some gruesome things would come on the screen I was about to forewarn him with: 'don't worry, this is only a film', when I realised that this was one time I couldn't say those words.

The findings on the global effects of any atomic war have been confirmed by scientists of all ideologies. They are convinced that there can be no victory in the event of a nuclear conflict because the consequent atmospheric changes will bring about what they now call a *Nuclear Winter* which will affect the whole earth. In fact I am uneasy about these films because somehow there is a danger that instead of heightening people's awareness they will numb the fears and allow us to drift into a fatal torpor.

For this reason McDonagh's book is particularly timely, since although people have become aware of the crisis, they shy away from analysing the causes. They seem to be defeated before they begin. The problem appears to be so great, and one that only governments can deal with, so what can the ordinary person do about it – beyond praying? It is at this point where McDonagh steps in and tells a different story. He shows us the roots of our present danger: spells out their implications and points to future remedies.

Though a sociologist and a theologian he is not remote from what he writes about. He lives in Mindanao in the southern Philippines. His daily life is passed in a struggle to prevent the destruction of the forests and the people he works with ... the T'boli tribe. As McDonagh unravels the causes we see that the T'boli are a symbol for the rest of us. Not only the T'boli but the whole human race stands in danger.

McDonagh is not just another voice condemning a twentieth-century lifestyle which exploits the earth's resources; on the contrary he brings us hope and a new direction. He draws together the ideas of a whole generation of like minds who have been working for a renewal of our respect for the earth, but he and his companions have, in collaboration with the T'boli people, taken up the challenge of working for solutions in the day-to-day life of the tribe. He shares this new *Pastorale* with us.

Some time ago, eight companions and I found ourselves in prison in the Philippines. Our allotted diet per day was five little fish (about two square inches in size) and two and a half cups of rice. Every second day there was also a liquid called soup. We succeeded, after various protests by the prisoners, in having that diet increased by 50 percent. The three peso a day food allowance was increased to four and a half pesos. The prison cook, knowing we had been involved in the protest, proudly produced the fish on the first day of the new diet; the size of each fish had doubled.

Now just at that time the media announced that interest rates in the US were about to go up. (This was due to new borrowings by the US government for the strategic defense initiative – Star Wars.) Simultaneously the next interest payment on the Philippine national debt (then standing at some twenty-five billion dollars) rose accordingly. A bridging loan of millions of dollars was needed immediately. The International Monetary Fund/World Bank insisted on the peso being devalued and prices rose. Within a couple of weeks the cook was back. Now *she* was the one protesting – the new allowance would not stretch: the fish shrank back to their old size. So finely tuned is the world economy today, that what happens in the First-World directly affects, within weeks, the diets of the Third-World. It is a small world. It is one world, and we are each other's keepers and we are keepers of the whole fragile earth which keeps us all.

It is understandable that we frequently succumb to the

temptation to allow to slip out of mind what is out of sight. We know that somewhere in Brazil tribal people are being hunted like game; we know of millions starving in Africa; we have heard that millions more are in refugee camps ... how many millions we are not sure. We have heard that the deserts are increasing and the rain forests disappearing; we have read that we have enough nuclear warheads to obliterate the human race several times over. But we don't connect these things. They seem to be disparate facts. Maybe we are subconsciously afraid to see how intimately connected they are, not just with each other, but with us. McDonagh has made it his task to look at the connections and face the fears.

The assault on the ecology of the Philippines will not cease with the passing of the Marcos era because it does not have its origin there. The same assault is going on worldwide throughout the whole earth. McDonagh examines the need for, and presents the outlines of, the deep spiritual change which must take place if we are to attack the roots and not just the symptoms. And this we must do because it is not 'the beauty of nature' which is in the balance but the survival of the human race.

Niall O'Brien
Maryknoll, 1986

For my mother

1

INTRODUCTION

The reflections in this study on ecology and religion arise from the unique possibilities afforded by the modern missionary venture. Until the second decade of this century a missionary left his or her homeland in Europe or North America with an already fashioned and completed Christian message, in order to preach that message to the peoples of Asia, Latin America, Africa and the Pacific. The chances of ever returning to his or her homeland were remote indeed.

During the heyday of western colonial expansion some missionaries showed a lively interest in the cultures of indigenous people of Asia, Africa and the Americas. Still, most Europeans would have been surprised if someone had suggested that the individual missionary might have something to learn from the people among whom he or she worked. A few may have conceded that, in order to survive in the torrid heat of the tropics, a missionary might do well to look to the customs and practices of the indigenous peoples. But it would have been considered unthinkable that the cultures of Africa, Asia, Latin America or the Pacific, and the insights gained in witnessing to the Christian faith there, might have something to contribute to a new and revitalized understanding of the Christian faith. Until the Second Vatican Council the missionary was seen as a person almost exclusively in a one-way communication stream. His or her task was to experience deeply and learn the tenets of the Christian faith in the West, and effectively communicate it elsewhere.

This image of the missionary has changed in recent decades. Sending missionaries to the other countries is no longer the exclusive domain of First – World Churches. Filipinos, Koreans, Indians and many other Christians from Third-World countries are now actively engaged in mission in many parts of the world. On another front the relative cheapness of international travel today means that all missionaries are likely to return to their Church of origin at regular intervals for holidays, for updating or to engage in missionary awareness programmes. When one adds the social, political, and economic changes in the world since World War II, the impact on the self-understanding and role of the missionary in the last two decades is profound.

From being in a one-way communication system, they are seen today as exchange agents. The missionary today strives to promote mutual understanding and enrichment among particular Churches by sharing experiences gained in a mission context with his or her Church of origin and *vice versa*. This is a particularly valuable service for First – World countries, as many missionaries, working in Third–World countries, are living in situations where people experience intensely some of the most important issues for the Church and the world, without the blurrings one often finds in First-World countries. This is particularly true of social inequality, which is so evident in the slums of Third-World cities. In this book I will argue that ecological destruction which is rampant, especially in tropical countries, is another such issue.

This book will attempt to share the way my own understanding of the shape and scope of my Christian faith has been fashioned, broadened and deepened by sixteen years working in Mindanao, in the Republic of the Philippines. Unless individuals decide to retreat into their own culture or religion and seal themselves off from the outside world, the environment in which they live affects their view of the world, including their faith. My assignments in Mindanao, first among lowland Christians, later in a Muslim area, and today among a tribal community called the T'boli have heightened my awareness of the need for a living faith in order to discern creatively what it means to be a Christian in today's world.

A decade and a half of missionary experience has focused my attention on three vital areas for the Church and world today. The first involves culture: How can a person be a disciple of Jesus within the context of his or her own culture, especially a non-western one? The second deals with justice: What are the demands of the Gospel of Jesus in a world where there is an ever-widening gap between rich and poor nations, and rich and poor people within the same country? The final question highlights the ecological crisis: How is a disciple of Jesus to respond to the rampant destruction and poisoning of the natural world which, if the current rate continues or increases, will threaten all life on Earth? This book will address itself to the last question, but first it might be helpful to place this discussion within the context of the Church's response in recent years to the other concerns.

Christians and Culture

My first assignment in Mindanao in the late 1960s and early 1970s was in a lowland Christian town in Misamis Occidental called Oroquieta. As my knowledge of the language and culture increased, I became increasingly aware of the fact that most of the symbols used to express and celebrate the Christian faith were western in origin and poorly adapted to the Filipino culture. Because the symbols and ecclesiastical language used in the liturgy were so foreign to the experience of ordinary people, they lacked the power to transform people's lives. I became more and more convinced of the need for culturally appropriate symbols and rituals, if the saving power of Christ was to touch the values and aspirations of a people in an extensive way.

I was not alone in my uneasiness. As a result of the prodding of missionary bishops and theologians, the Fathers of the Second Vatican Council recognized the need for the Church to enter deeply into the culture and religious experience of diverse peoples, especially of non-western ones. The Council document on the Missions (*Ad Gentes*) exhorts missionaries to have 'a great respect for the patrimony, language and cultures of the people among whom they work' (No. 26).

This awareness of the need to inculturate the Gospel has gained momentum in recent years in all the Christian Churches. Conferences and meetings have been held in

Bangkok (1972–3), Nairobi (1973) and Melbourne (1980).
Consultations among evangelical Churches took place at
Willowbank and a Synod on Evangelization was held in Rome
in 1974. In *Evangelii Nuntiandi* – the document to emerge
from that Synod – Pope Paul VI stressed the need for
inculturation in clear terms: 'The split between the Gospel and
culture is without doubt the drama of our times, just as it was
of other times. Therefore, every effort must be made to ensure
a full evangelization of culture, or more correctly, cultures'
(EN 20).[1]

So in the past twenty years some steps have been taken to
inculturate the Gospel in local cultures. The first stage
involved the translation of the Lectionary and Sacramentary
and other liturgical texts into local languages. There have been
bumps on the road. It has proved much more difficult to move
from translating Latin texts to celebrating the Christian
mysteries in an appropriate local symbolic idiom. For one
thing, the creativity needed does not emerge overnight. It
takes time, patience and experimentation. It is also not easy
for those working in the Roman Curia to set aside the
centralizing tendencies of a thousand years, particularly when
it means whittling away at their own power. A number of
documents coming from Rome in recent years – most notably
Inaestimabile Donum,[2] and the recent *Instruction On Certain
Aspects Of The Theology Of Liberation*[3] from the Congregation
for Doctrine and Faith – have attempted to put the brakes on
experimentation in the area of ministry, theological reflection
and liturgy. Still, despite these setbacks, it is true to say that
more and more Christians today are struggling with the task of
how to express and celebrate their faith in a meaningful way.

Christians and Social Justice

While cultural differences are often subtle, nuanced and
difficult to recognize at first glance, there was nothing subtle
about the poverty which struck me so forcibly on my arrival in
Manila in 1969. The human anguish which poverty causes
individuals and families was reinforced each time I saw a
family group arrive at the Church door with the body of a dead

infant or young child. It added flesh and blood to the cold statistics I had read on the rate of infant mortality. In almost every case the death resulted from gastro-enteritis or a malnutrition-related disease which could easily have been cured if the parents had had access to medical care and nutritious food.

Gradually, the global dimension of poverty and its continual expansion began to dawn on me. A few statistics capture something of the gigantic nature of this challenge to humanity. In 1984, 2.1 billion people, or 46 percent of the world's population were living in varying degrees of poverty. World Bank figures calculate that over 800 million people live in dire poverty, with all the severe illness and deprivation which flow from poverty. Some 2.1 billion people do not have access to clean water, while 1.5 billion lack any effective medical care.

Church documents like *Populorum Progressio*,[4] *The Apostolic Letter to Cardinal Roy*,[5] the statement of the 1971 Synod of Bishops, *Justice in the World*,[6] and the insights of liberation theologians living and working in Latin America helped me and many other Christians to understand that the poverty of Third-World countries is not an isolated phenomenon. It is not caused by the indolence of the poor or by religious fatalism, though many people in First-World countries would like us to believe this. These documents insist that the poverty which is affecting more and more of the world's population is directly related to the misuse and squandering of natural and human resources in First–World – mostly traditionally Christian – countries. The life-style and consumption patterns of many people in First-World countries are way beyond what the Earth can support, and can only be maintained by enslaving the vast majority of the world's population.

The most prominent symbol of this prodigious waste is, of course, the suicidal arms race which is progressively gobbling up more and more natural resources. For example, when I arrived in the Philippines in 1969, the bill world-wide for military spending was $236 billion. In 1983 it had risen to $650 billion and it is still constantly rising, fuelled mainly by irrational fears. In the United States alone the money squandered on arms exports from 1968 to 1982 escalated from $1 billion to $21 billion. Equally saddening is the misuse of human resources. Fifty percent of the world's one million scientists are involved one way or another with the military. To put it in human terms, there are two and a half times as many military personnel as health workers.

A fraction of the vast financial, technological, natural and human resources which are now devoted to military purposes, if channelled into productive use in agriculture, health, social, and economic development programmes, would significantly improve the standard of living of millions of people. This in turn would reduce many local and global tensions. Today, and more so in the future, the threat to peace on a local and global level will not come from human disagreements, but from the deteriorating relationship between human beings and the natural world that nourishes us. This is very true here in Mindanao and in places like El Salvador in Central America. Even what is called the insurgency problem can, at root, be traced to the depletion of land, and the movement of settlers into tribal areas due both to the entry of large agribusiness corporations and a major increase in population. Unless we face up to this squarely – increasing arms production is heightening rather than solving the problem – the scramble for scarce resources will set off more local conflicts, which may become global.

Third-World elites, and especially those in power in Third-World countries, cannot be exonerated from blame for the growing poverty of their people. A combination of incompetence, mismanagement, grandiose and useless projects and outright corruption has crippled many economies and saddled the countries with enormous foreign debts. The extravagance of the Marcos regime in the Philippines is legendary. When Manila was chosen to host the 1976 IMF-World Bank conference, the government spent $200 million building luxury hotels to impress the foreigners. Scarce money was poured into a Heart Center in Manila, though cardiovascular diseases are not common among ordinary Filipinos, while health care for the most prevalent diseases is woefully inadequate. A Heart Center and luxury hotels, though inappropriate, given the poverty of the Philippines, might make some economic sense but it is difficult to justify the pouring of money into building an experimental Film Center in Manila.

Apart from misspent money, charges of corruption among government officials are rife in many Third-World countries, including the Philippines. Just one example of corruption in the sugar industry in the mid-1970s will suffice. Alfred McCoy in *Priests on Trial*[7] points out that even during the slump in the price of sugar on the international markets, the Marcos administration continued to build seven new sugar mills, though this ran counter to all sane business advice. Given the bleak future prospects for the sugar industry at the time, the deal only made sense when it was revealed that Marubeni Corporation – the Japanese firm supplying the mills – paid $6 million dollars commission per mill to relatives and cronies of people in the administration.

During the regime of President Marcos, beginning in 1965, all the indices of poverty increased in the Philippines, while the foreign debt ballooned from $500 million to over $26 billion. Much of the money borrowed from foreign banks never reached the country. In July 1985 *Mercury News*, a daily newspaper in Northern California, published a three-part series listing Filipinos who owned property or business in the United States. Most of the people named, including ex-President and Mrs Marcos, are associated with the previous administration. The money which has been channelled into the United States economy runs into billions, a significant percentage of the Philippines foreign debt.

While it assuages the conscience of First-World people to concentrate on this aspect of the poverty treadmill, the greater share of the blame for the increase of poverty in our world must rest squarely on the shoulders of the 'developed' countries. The social, economic, political and military policies pursued in the United States, western Europe, Japan, and the USSR marginalize significant minorities in these countries and condemn the vast majority of human beings to increased poverty. In the United States, for example, a 1984 report drawn up by the Congressional Research and Budget Office noted that there has been a 50 percent increase in poverty among children since the 1960s. One child in four now lives in a family below the poverty line.

The miserly aid, which so many First-World leaders boast about, has also been very much reduced in recent years. The Thatcher government in Britain has slashed the overseas aid budget by eight percent in real terms since 1979. Only far-reaching changes in First–World countries themselves however, especially in the international economic and trading system, will reverse the growing disparity between the rich and poor nations.

The world economic situation today is particularly embarrassing for Christians. The 1.5 billion followers of Jesus, 'who had no place to lay his head', now control two thirds of the Earth's resources and, on average, are three times better off than their non-Christian neighbours. Fortunately, there are signs that attitudes are beginning to change. During the past two decades some Christians in the 'developed' world are beginning to respond to the challenge of their brothers and sisters in 'developing' countries. They are becoming more aware of the legacy of colonialism. This formed the basis of much of the West's wealth while it often impoverished Third-World countries. They now feel challenged to work for a new, more just, international economic order which will redistribute the world's resources in order to ensure that every person in the world has enough of the world's goods to live a decent human life.

Ecological Devastation

The third major challenge which I see facing our world today has to do with the progressive destruction of the natural world. This is very clearly evident in Mindanao. My attention has been drawn more and more to this since I began working with the T'boli people five years ago. The T'boli are a tribal people, about 70,000 in all, who today live in the southeastern part of Mindanao in the mountains of South Cotabato. They have lost, and continue to lose, much of their traditional ancestral territory to lowland Filipinos from the northern and central part of the country who, in recent decades, have migrated to Mindanao. In common with 200 million tribal people spread around the world, they are at the bottom of the socio-economic ladder. Besides being stalked by poverty, malnutrition and disease, they face the prospect of cultural extinction unless the forces that are destroying them are kept at bay. The threat of extinction comes not because their culture is disintegrating through internal pressures, but because their environment – the rain forest – is rapidly being destroyed both through commercial cutting of trees by loggers and the agricultural practices of lowland peasants in search of scarce land.

In the T'boli hills one becomes conscious of the fragility of what is often considered to be a luxuriant environment. Where the tropical forest bloomed in the very recent past, I see today eroded and scarred hills which will only support cogon grass. When I move down from the hill to the plains of South Cotabato I see huge monocrop plantations growing pineapples and bananas. Once again severe erosion caused by torrential rain, wind and sun ensures a very limited life-span for these plantations. The massive use of pesticides, insecticides and herbicides further depletes and poisons the soil. As I drive by, one question is always on my mind – where are the people going to get land on which to grow food? Above all, where are the children and future generations going to grow the food that they will need for an expanding population if these fertile lands are turned into deserts? Even if the birth rate falls substantially in the Philippines over the next few decades, experts project that the present population of 54.9 million will reach beyond 70 million by the year 2000.

Further down the coast I see marine resources being squandered and destroyed. Mangrove swamps and coral reefs, the breeding grounds for a variety of fish, are dynamited, over-fished, drained and destroyed. Fish and rice are now staple food for many Filipinos. Yet the supply of fish will dry up unless these destructive practices are reversed.

As I witness this destruction of the natural world and read numerous authoritative reports on the deepening ecological crisis in First-World countries, I am more and more convinced that both human beings and the other members of the Earth community have reached a critical point. We can no longer take the natural world for granted as if it will always be there unchanged. The first thing we must do is to recognize the damage that our profit-oriented approach to the world has already caused and begin to care actively for the dynamic stability and regenerative powers of the Earth. Famine in

Ethiopia gives us a glimpse of what life might be like for countless millions in the future if the fertility of the Earth is impaired. While the long drought is the immediate cause of the famine, over-grazing or inappropriate agriculture has eroded topsoil and turned once-fertile land into desert. In every region of the world human beings need to discover a new, less exploitative relationship with the natural world.

In our efforts to seek this new relationship, religion must play a significant role. It must help us to recapture much of the respect and reverence which earlier generations had for the natural world. There is, however, no way we can simply return to some idealized rustic past and forget the knowledge of the world which modern science has communicated to us. In fact these insights into the physical, biological and spiritual emergencies of our Earth can help us to go beyond the respect our ancestors had for the world. We see in the beauty and diversity of the myriad life-forms a wonderful, interrelated community which is fruitful if cared for, but which proves fragile when abused. It is a world that evokes awe, reverence, gratitude and prudent use, traditionally called husbandry. The natural world is important for every religious tradition. In its beauty and abundance it is the primary revelation of God to all men and women. Like tribal people around the world, we too must once again commune with God in nature.

I think it is true to say that while in recent years many Christians and Christian leaders have begun to respond to the challenge posed by culture and social justice, few have as yet responded to the challenge of the ecological crisis. True, Christian leaders often condemn the spirit of acquisitiveness and rampant materialism which co-exists with appalling poverty among millions of people in the modern world. But even when the issue is raised—as it is in Pope Paul VI's *Apostolic Letter to Cardinal Roy*[8] or in Pope John Paul II's speech in Nairobi on 18 August 1985 at the United Nations Centre for the Environment[9]—the problem is looked upon exclusively from a human perspective; hence it fails to reveal the extent of the damage to the total Earth community. As we will see, is not an adequate framework within which to grasp the magnitude and multi-faceted dimension of the ecological crisis which is poisoning vast amounts of water, contaminating the air and depleting topsoil, ensuring desolation for all the creatures of the Earth in the future. Because the understanding of the problem is not adequate, religious leaders cannot plumb the depths of their religious traditions in a way that will help believers face this problem and galvanize them to do something about it before it is too late.

They also seem to be unaware of the challenge which a deteriorating environment poses for the Christian faith itself. Father Thomas Berry, who calls himself a geologian and is the director of the Riverdale Center for Religious Research in New York, states what is involved for the Christian Churches in a recent comment:

> My question is: After we burn the lifeboat how will we stay afloat? Presently the Church has a unique opportunity to place its vast authority, its energies, educational resources, its spiritual disciplines in a creative context, one that can assist in renewing the Earth as a bio-spiritual planet. If this is not done immediately, then by the end of century an overwhelming amount of damage will have been done, an immense number of living species will be irrevocably lost for all future generations. Only by assuming this religious responsibility for the fate of the Earth can the Church regain any authentic status either in the human or in the Earth process.[10]

To Care For The Earth

If present trends continue, by the turn of the century we will face an environmental catastrophe as irreversible as any nuclear holocaust. Part 1 of this book will state the nature and extent of this problem and draw up a framework for understanding what is happening. I will begin in Chapter 2 with some general observations on ecology and a bird's-eye-view of the damage to water, air, soil, and genetic diversity. The perspective will attempt to be global, though many examples will be taken from the Philippines. Chapter 3 will discuss ecological problems in Ireland. These are two countries with which I am familiar, since I was born and went to school in Ireland, and for 16 years I have worked and have been educated in the Philippines. Having looked at what is happening in a Third-World and First-World country today, in Chapter 4 I will outline a history of the present malaise and our attitudes to it.

I will argue that since the Enlightenment period, Christians have no longer possessed a comprehensive *story of the universe* to guide them in their relationship with the Earth. This lacuna is particularly tragic as it coincided with the aggressive, exploitative expansion of western colonialism and the increased power of modern technology to reprocess, and in many ways destroy, the natural world. When in the late eighteenth, nineteenth and twentieth centuries scientific discoveries began to describe a new story of how the universe and the community of the living emerged, there was little religious reflection on the significance of the new insights. This was unfortunate as it could have guided modern western society, and especially its technology, down a different path in relation to the natural world, one marked by awe, wonder, praise and responsibility rather than by plunder.

Part 1 ends with a chapter entitled *The New Story*. This synthesis, which is based on the writings of Teilhard de Chardin and Thomas Berry, is the pivotal chapter of the book.

Part 2 attempts to draw out the implications of this new story of the universe for the Christian theology of creation. Three chapters are devoted to this. Chapter 6 looks at the biblical tradition, while Chapter 7 examines some of the ways in which the Christian message has been lived out over the centuries and which have been both respectful and destructive of the natural world. I call this the bright and dark side of the Christian tradition. Chapter 8 discusses how our theology of creation can be enriched by the teachings and lived traditions of other faiths. Chapters 9, 10, 11 and 12 discuss the implications of this enriched theology of creation for liturgy, the sacraments, Christian moral living, spirituality and mission. Data from ecologically oriented sciences form the backbone of much of the first Part, while reflections based on theological sources are at the heart of the second Part. However, there is no clear division between theological and scientific observations. Both are intertwined, following the model of Teilhard de Chardin himself, since both are at the heart of the New Story.

The book ends with a brief reflection on the missionary implications of the New Story. In this way, the circle is complete. The reflection began in a missionary context and eventually returns there. Witnessing to the Gospel of Jesus, concern for a more just social order, and care for the Earth go hand in hand.

PART ONE

THE THREAT TO LIFE ON EARTH

2

SPOILING THE EARTH

The word ecology is derived from the Greek word, *oikos*, which means 'house' or 'place in which to live'. According to Eugene Odum in *Fundamentals of Ecology*,[1] it is literally the study of organisms 'at home'. Included in this 'at home' is the study of living beings, the place in which they live, and the interaction among and between the living and non-living components of the place being studied. So ecology attempts to understand the complex web of linkages, relationships and interdependencies in a particular environment or ecosystem. The ecosystem being studied might be a meadow, a freshwater lake, a mangrove swamp, an island, a continent, an ocean or finally the Earth itself.

Ecology reminds us that human beings are part of the 'house'. During the past few million years, as we will see in Chapter 4, we have evolved with the Earth. We deceive ourselves if we ever think we can survive without the Earth. If, however, we continue to ignore the Earth as we are doing now, we may bring the whole house down around our ears.

As an emerging discipline, ecology combines insights from numerous sciences: biology, genetics, biochemistry, zoology, chemistry, geology and geography. Its particular focus is not on the properties of a single organism, but on the interrelations between living forms and their environment. The hallmark of the study is its relational, dynamic perspective.

Ecosystems are never completely static; they are dynamic realities. Nevertheless most ecosystems in their natural environment develop a dynamic stability unless significant changes are introduced from the outside to disrupt the pattern of relationships. In some situations, outside influences are so massive that an ecosystem collapses. Eutrophication is a case in point; high concentrations of nitrogen and phosphorus entering a body of fresh water can induce a proliferation of algae which suffocate many of the traditional life-forms in the lake and leave the lake itself biologically 'dead'. When the focus of study widens from a single ecosystem to the Earth itself, many ecologists fear that the changes presently taking place in the biosphere – the air, water and thin layer of soil that is essential for all life on earth – are so massive that they will cause the collapse, or serious depletion, of essential ecosystems like the oceans, with disastrous consequences for all life-forms, including human beings.

At this moment in history ecology has much to teach each of us as individuals and as a human family so that we may begin to care more for the only home we all share – planet Earth.

There is a problem with the word ecology itself. While its etymology aptly describes what needs to be done to understand, care for and preserve our home, it shares the fate of many other Greek-derived nouns in English. It sounds technical and abstract and fails to evoke a warm response among ordinary non-technical people. Something like 'life-community', or 'the community of the living', or 'Earth community' might have more emotionally attractive over-tones, and thus awaken more people to the fact that our home is under attack. The enemy, unfortunately, is within and not always easy to understand or combat. It may come as a surprise, for example, that religious beliefs can spawn behaviour which is destructive of the Earth without evoking a twinge of conscience. Christians who see salvation exclusively as an other-world reality are often not challenged in their faith by injustice among people or by the destruction of the Earth.

Poisoning the Earth

The interconnectedness and interrelatedness of all living and non-living forms is, according to Barry Commoner in *The Closing Circle*,[2] the primary law of ecology. This is why we must be particularly careful about what we spray on crops, because the crops that we spray will end up on our tables and poison us. Take the well-shaped and nutritious-looking fruit neatly arranged in the fruit bowl: unfortunately, it may not be as wholesome as it appears on the outside. Vast amounts of pesticides and additives – many toxic chemicals – are used both in growing and ripening the fruit. In California alone, in 1980, three hundred million pounds of pesticides were used. It is estimated that 20 percent of the total went into producing what is called the 'cosmetic effect' so that the fruit will look attractive and fetch premium prices on the supermarket shelves.

Chemicals have been used in agriculture for the last forty years. At first they were greeted favourably by almost everyone as they yielded bumper harvests. Soon, however, it was realized that constant use of chemicals destroys the long-term natural fertility of soil. For one thing they are not selective in the organisms they kill; as well as killing organisms considered pests by the farmer, they destroy organisms which are beneficial to the soil and which naturally control pests. Pesticides kill earthworms which are some of the farmer's best friends, as they play an important role in fertilizing and aerating the soil. Pesticides also leach vital metallic nutrients such as phosphorus, potassium, iron and manganese from the soil.

The health hazards arising from pesticides are now being appreciated by people in First-World countries. For this reason many are banned or severely restricted. They are known to cause cancer, genetic disorders, sterility, skin allergies and emphysema. Unfortunately, the poison may remain active in the soil long after the original spraying; organochloride pesticides like DDT remain active in the soil for years. They continue to pass their poison through the food chain and are now found in the Arctic region in the fatty tissue of fish and birds that have never had direct contact with the chemical.

Some controls have been introduced in First-World countries, but fruit, vegetables or other agricultural produce grown in plantations owned by multinational corporations in Third-World countries may have been sprayed by dangerous

chemicals which are either banned or strictly controlled in
First-World countries. These chemicals are readily available,
in fact are often dumped, on Third-World markets. Many
chemical companies, seeing their pesticide market levelling off
in First-World countries, have begun to bombard Third-
World countries and pressurize their governments to relax
restrictions on the export of dangerous chemicals. One of the
first acts of the Reagan administration in 1980 was to rescind
an order by his predecessor Jimmy Carter, banning the export
of hazardous substances.[3] In another dangerous development,
many chemical manufacturers, hungry for business, have
hastily assembled agrochemical plants in Third-World
countries. These are often faulty and poorly managed, paving
the way for the tragic events that the world witnessed in
Bhopal, India, in December 1984.

Third-World workers are very poorly protected against
pesticide poisoning. Here in Mindanao I see farmers spraying
crops almost every day without any protective clothing.
Though many develop lung diseases and skin allergies from
inhaling the fumes, the damage is often done before they link
their ailment with chemical spraying. Manufacturers aggres-
sively advertise their products. They promise a 'miracle' yield
to the farmer but fail to mention the long-term dangers which
are associated with using chemicals. They do not tell the
farmer that pesticides poison fish and molluscs which are a
traditional source of protein in the rural areas. There is very
little effort made to encourage the farmers to take precautions
when using chemicals. Very often, farmers are ignorant of the
side-effects of the chemicals.

In large-scale plantations, the plight of the workers is often
worse. Many of the agribusinesses in Mindanao, in South
Cotabato and Bukidnon, spray their pineapples and bananas
from the air. Flagmen on the ground who direct the pilots, and
even the people living in the bunk-houses close by are
poisoned by the spray.

Pesticide-related diseases are becoming a major health
hazard in Third-World countries. Oxfam estimates that each
year there are now around 750,000 cases of pesticide poisoning
in Third-World countries. Not everyone affected by the
poisoning dies, but the health of a considerable percentage of

the population is being impaired. Maurice Strong, the former head of the United Nations Environmental Programme, estimates that a farm worker in Central America carries about eleven times more DDT residue in his body tissue than his average North American counterpart.

This practice of dumping substances which are considered unsafe to use at home on Third-World countries is callous, immoral and also myopic. Many countries affected export farm produce to the United States. With the fruit and vegetables come the toxic chemicals which, in turn, will poison the citizens of the United States. This circle of poison is a neat and deadly illustration of the links between all living beings.

To summarize what I have been saying thus far: during the past forty years we have been progressively poisoning the body of nature in almost every corner of the globe. Without any extensive knowledge about the harmful long-term effects of these chemicals, we have tampered with the delicate balance of nature, ensuring in many areas problems greater than crop pests.

Fortunately people have begun to take action to remedy the damage. In the United States, the Environmental Defense Fund is campaigning for more restrictions and better controls on the use of chemicals. On the international level, an organization called PAN (Pesticide Action Network) was set up in the wake of a global conference on pesticide trade in Malaysia in 1982. This organization encourages farmers to return to the traditional biological methods for controlling pests. It disseminates information on the harmful effects of chemicals and campaigns for legislation to control their manufacture, export and use. They prepare educational kits for schools, farmers' organizations and consumer groups.

Another one of Commoner's laws of ecology – everything must go somewhere – is a slight variation on the theme of interrelatedness. What is excreted by one organism or system is taken up by another as food. There is no escaping from the processes of the food chain. Plants, through solar energy, convert the non-living world into living tissue; animals feed on plants and on each other. Humans are part of the animal world and so consume plants and animals.

There are, unfortunately, many examples of the tragic consequences of not taking this law seriously. The inappropriate use of pesticides is one, as they do not readily disintegrate into non-toxic forms. Industrial pollution in Minamata Bay in Japan is another well-known example. Over the years, factories have discharged mercury-contaminated water into the Minamata Bay. Gradually, the mercury passed through the food chain and eventually accumulated in edible fish. At least 10,000 people who have eaten seafood from the area are now experiencing varying degrees of disability. Some are paralysed completely, others are suffering from varying degrees of blindness or chronic headaches. Deaths from what is now known as the Minamata disease have already exceeded six hundred.

Industrial Pollution

This kind of industrial pollution is not confined to First-World industrialized countries. I spent five years from 1976 to 1981 as chaplain at the Mindanao State University in Marawi City on the island of Mindanao. In the nearby coastal city of Iligan there is a host of polluting industries, including two cement factories, which pollute the air. These are responsible for a significant rise in respiratory diseases. A steel works also discharges dust into the air and pollutes the bay with acids and chemicals involved in the steel-making process. A vinyl plant produces caustic soda, hydrochloride and polyvinyl chloride. Preliminary findings from scientists at the Iligan Institute of Technology indicate that the present level of mercury in fish and other aquatic organisms in the bay is above the tolerable level. This leads people to believe that the vinyl plant surreptitiously discharges mercury into the bay. Also in the area to make up the coterie of dirty industries are *Maria Christina Chemical Industries, Inc.*, and *Refractories Corporation of the Philippines.*[4]

Much of our industrial pollution stems from a 'flush it down the toilet' approach. Once the harmful substance is out of sight, people tend to forget about it. This 'out of sight, out of mind' attitude, so common today, is very dangerous. Invariably our actions return to haunt us. Another of

Commoner's laws tells us that 'there is no free lunch'. This comes as a shock, as we are used to dumping things, preferably in other people's backyard. Now we know that someone must pay the cost. Unfortunately, the persons who are called on to pay the cost, in terms of damage to their own health or environment, are often not the people who caused the mess in the first place.

Acid rain illustrates this cycle very well. In the United States, England, Germany, Japan and other industrial states it was decided that one way to combat smog, which was so much a feature of industrial city life, was to encourage industries to build taller smoke stacks. The taller stacks may help reduce the smog in the vicinity of the plant, but they cause serious problems to freshwater lakes, forests, and farmlands hundreds of miles away. While solving one immediate pollution problem, the tall stacks cause another. They keep vanadium traces, which are found in coal and released on combustion, in contact with sulphur dioxide for a longer period and inject them into the atmosphere at a higher level. In North America and Europe the prevailing winds carry the sulphur dioxide and nitrogen oxides over Canada and Scandinavia, respectively, and transform them on the way. When they react with water vapour they turn into nitric and sulphuric acid and fall to the ground with rain or snow. This rain is sometimes as acidic as vinegar.

Thousands of freshwater lakes in Canada and Scandinavia are now so acidic that all life-forms are dying. In Sweden alone 18,000 lakes out of a total of 96,000 are affected. The increased acidity of the soil is destroying the Black Forest. Since the Black Forest is so important for German mythology, acid rain has become a political issue in Germany. The destruction of the forest is also having a damaging impact on the German timber industry. Acid rain is also damaging relations between Canada and the United States. Canadian scientists estimate that more than 4.5 million tonnes of acid reaching eastern Canada originate in the United States. The Reagan administration is dragging its heels by insisting on more scientific studies before effectively tackling the source of the problem by limiting the emissions from heavy industries and coal burning utilities in the United States.

An international conference was held on acid rain in Munich in July 1984. Eighteen of the participating nations, recognizing the seriousness of the problem, agreed to reduce their emissions of sulphur dioxide by 30 percent over the next five years. Predictably enough, both the Thatcher government and the Reagan administration refused to sign. As these are among the major culprits, there is little hope for reduction in acid rain in the years ahead. Inactivity will not banish the problem; somebody will have to pay, and pay heavily, as the noxious gases poison the air, destroy woodlands and kill off the fish.

The Philippines and the Third-World countries have yet to experience acid rain on the scale that is now affecting industrialized countries. Sadly, however, the Philippines is quickly catching up. Two years ago when I was attending a conference in Taytay just outside Manila, I could see a pollution smog settling on the city each afternoon. The National Pollution Control Commission (NPCC) estimated that in 1979, 400 tonnes of pollutants from motor vehicles and industrial plants were discharged into the atmosphere each day.

Acid rain points once again to the connections between all things. Spewing toxic substances into the air does not merely damage the air we breathe, it also contaminates the water, and affects woodlands and the soil.

Global 2000: a warning

Fortunately some people are beginning to wake up to what is happening. One indication of this is the growing interest in ecology right round the world. This is not simply confined to ecologists and biologists. The ecology movement is mainly composed of ordinary men and women who are worried about the quality of the environment in which they and their children will have to live. They realize that the modern industrial, consumer society is progressively damaging the biosphere. Unless this damage is arrested and reversed it will permanently damage the quality of life and even the conditions necessary for life on Earth. Doctors, scientists, artists and popular musicians have taken up the theme.

Eric Bogle, the popular Australian folk-singer, has recorded many songs on environmental issues. One of his latest records is an anti-nuclear song entitled *When the Wind Blows*. On the same record he laments the poisoning of rivers in a poignant song called *Shining River*. A recent Doug Ashdown and Jimmy Stewart record has a song about denuding the forest called *Places The Trees Should Have Grown*.

Unfortunately, many politicians who are aware of the challenge which a growing ecological movement poses to industrial society, attempt to caricature it as an esoteric pursuit by harmless but misguided drop-outs, engaged in protecting endangered species like the Snail Darter in the United States or the Daintree forest in Northern Queensland. The truth, however, is that many of the people raising the hue and cry are compassionate and caring men and women with a high degree of scientific competence. The long list includes René Dubos, Barbara Ward, Amory Lovins, Lester Brown, Erik Eckholm, Carl Sagan, Paul and Anne Ehrlich and a host of others.

Their worries about what is happening to the biosphere and the consequences for the future of the planet are backed by an immense body of scientific literature at both the popular and technical level, which is both sobering and disturbing.

At the moment, much of the data on which the scientists base their warnings and predictions is now available in a single authoritative study called *The Global 2000 Report to the President*.[5] The report was commissioned by President Carter and compiled using the vast technical resources of international agencies and many US government departments. The cover of the Penguin paperback edition features a paint brush indicating that, while certain details are still fuzzy and may not be completely accurate, owing to lack of reliable data or an inadequate conceptual model, the main message is both clear and disturbing. Another extremely well-prepared single volume work on the same theme is *Gaia: An Atlas Of Planet Management*.[6] This is a very informative and easy-to-use reference work with maps and charts and illustrations which tell, almost at a glance, what is happening to our air, land, water, marine life, food and other living forms on planet Earth. Many of the examples which I use in this book come from these two very important studies.

What do they tell us? The message is simple but very revolutionary. Humans have not learned to live creatively within the constraints of the biosphere. Since the dawn of history, but particularly in the past two hundred years, men and women have acted as if the system was infinite, inexhaustible and ever resilient. People felt that there were always new frontiers beyond the horizon to explore and exploit. These studies insist that we must abandon that way of thinking and acting. The bottom line is not the profits a company makes this year or next year, but the fact that we live on a planet with finite, limited resources that can be irretrievably lost. If we continue to poison our land, air and water and waste our timber, mineral and other natural resources we are heading full speed towards disaster for all life forms on Earth, including ourselves. The letter of transmittal to President Carter included in the text of *Global 2000* summarizes the concern of the authors. It states that 'there is a potential for global problems of alarming proportions by the year 2000'. They go on to predict that, unless decisive action is taken through caring for the Earth, with widespread, tough conservation measures and pollution controls, we will see a 'progressive degradation and impoverishment of the Earth's resources in the years to come'.

In discussing some of the basic tenets of ecology we have seen the damage which industrial and agricultural pollution is causing to the Earth. There are other ways in which human activity is damaging the self-renewing systems which make life on Earth possible and bountiful. Looked at over the long term, it is clear that mankind, through modern industrial processes, is progressively shutting off the power for many of the renewable life-systems of Earth. To sustain industrial societies we are destroying the colour, beauty and diversity of the Earth and creating instead a lonely, monotonous and desolate Earth. This surely is exchanging the birthright of all the living for a mess of pottage for a relatively small number of humans!

Air Pollution

Humans are bringing about changes in the atmosphere which can affect the global climate. A temperature change of a few degrees one way or another is all that is needed to bring about a new ice age or to melt the polar icecaps. The climatic changes which might be expected to follow from temperature change will adversely affect some of the world's most fertile agricultural lands. Even a slight change in rainfall patterns in the American mid-West and Canada could have a disastrous effect on food production in the area. Significantly reduced grain harvests in North America would cause widespread famine in many parts of the world.

How are we causing these changes? Carbon dioxide in the atmosphere has increased by 30 percent since 1850. In the 1970s about 15 billion tonnes of carbon dioxide were injected into the atmosphere each year, mainly through industrial activity, coal burning, car exhausts and inorganic fertilizer. Since increased carbon dioxide causes a 'greenhouse' effect – it captures solar heat which otherwise would be reflected back to space – it is expected that there will be a temperature rise of 2 to 4 degrees Celsius during the early decades of the next century. The rise in the polar region could be as high as 6 degrees Celsius. Such a warming of the Earth's atmosphere will lead to a significant rise in the level of the oceans and therefore cause widespread flooding in coastal plains and many of the world's most densely populated cities such as London, New York, Manila, to mention only three.

There is also a worrying threat to the ozone region from a number of quarters. The ozone region protects higher animals such as ourselves from skin cancer. It is much more important for micro-organisms like plankton whose reproductive processes will be seriously impaired or even destroyed if the ozone region is depleted. The damage to this region comes mainly from three sources. The enormous increase in nitrogen fertilizer in recent years releases nitrous oxide into the atmosphere. This eats away at the ozone region. High oil prices may have saved us from the second area of concern which is supersonic aircraft. Supersonic flying has proved to be prohibitively expensive. The third prong in the attack is still very active. It comes from chlorofluorocarbons which are used mainly as propellant substances for aerosol cans and as refrigerants.

In the Philippines air pollution is mainly concentrated in cities. I have already referred to the industrial smog that hangs over Metro Manila each day. Many of the 800 industrial centres pollute the air. Uncontrolled vehicle emissions are also a major factor in the rise of pulmonary tuberculosis, pneumonia and bronchitis in urban areas.

One of the most worrying features about atmospheric pollution world-wide, like the increase in carbon dioxide in the air and the effect of chlorofluorocarbons on the ozone region, is that we really do not know what will happen. In a sense we are the ones gambling with the destiny of the next generation and all succeeding generations. We are subjecting them to an experiment which may have disastrous consequences. By the time the scale of the changes involved become clear to us, for example if the polar icecaps begin to melt, it will be too late to do much to arrest the damage. Not even the most addicted gambler is playing for such high stakes and many of our political leaders and industrial planners are not even aware of what is involved!

Soil Erosion

Plant life is absolutely dependent on a thin, fragile layer of topsoil. Nothing will grow on land without this precious resource, yet, through a whole battery of destructive agricultural practices, human beings are depleting the soil and causing massive erosion. It is estimated that 75 billion tonnes are lost world-wide each year. Asia has the distinction of being the worst affected area. It loses 25 billion tonnes annually. It also has the highest population. These two trends in collision are a recipe for disaster. First–World countries are not immune. The United States loses 5 billion tonnes, mainly in the wheat-growing areas. Added to that, over 4 million hectares of arable land are lost each year in the United States to urban sprawl, shopping malls and highway construction. Australia is also badly hit, losing 5 tonnes per hectare in wheat-growing areas. This has meant that over the years much of Australia's agricultural land has become degraded.

The loss of topsoil has reached disastrous proportions in many Third-World tropical countries. With the destruction of the rain forest, the fragile topsoil is quickly eroded by the wind, sun and torrential rain, especially during the monsoons. The Bureau of Soil in the Philippines estimates that over 500 million tonnes are eroded annually. Of the 30 million hectares which comprise the land area of the Philippines, 8.5 million hectares are now seriously eroded. With a growing population and little serious planning to conserve land, the outlook is not very bright for the millions who are already living near starvation level today.

The destruction of topsoil in the Third-World countries due to erosion, overgrazing, inappropriate methods of farming and salinization is very worrying. A growing number of countries can no longer feed their people. Today the focus is on Africa, where land which was formerly productive is being turned into desert at an alarming rate. The extensive famine raging there is a direct result of the misuse of land. The emaciated bodies of men, women and children which are captured so strikingly by our TV cameras are a grim reminder of what may be in store for hundreds of millions of people in Africa, Latin America and Asia unless remedial action on an extensive scale is taken immediately.

According to a recent global assessment by the United Nations Environmental Program, this problem of desertification is becoming extremely serious. Each year, eleven million hectares of productive land are turned into desert. The same report further warns that 35 percent of the world's arable land is in danger of being turned into desert unless the problem is recognized and faced in a serious way.

In the Philippines, deserts have engulfed almost 400 hectares of land which was formerly lush tropical forest on the island of Luzon, in Ilocos Norte and Ilocos Sur. Indiscriminate cutting of the forest for firewood and for curing tobacco was the culprit in those areas. Those deserts are spreading rapidly, and signs of impending desertification are evident in the Visayas – the islands in the central Philippines – and also in Mindanao.

High salinity and waterlogging also renders land unproductive. These are often by-products of massive irrigation projects. Initially the irrigation brings dry land, which formerly could not be cultivated, into production. However, unless there is also good drainage, waterlogging and salinization can soon render this land useless. On a train journey from Lahore to Karachi in Pakistan one sees field after field which has had to be abandoned because of the high salinity of the soil.

Land is a finite resource, so the present exploitative approach to it cannot continue much longer. Many people aptly describe modern agriculture as 'soil mining'. We are digging into the capital that the Earth has prepared over millions of years. We easily forget that the soil that is lost so quickly takes hundreds, in some situations, thousands of years to build up. No machine has been devised to create fertile soil. If we are going to feed adequately a population of eleven billion people by the mid-twenty-first century, then we will need to care for soil by using farming methods which enrich rather than abuse it. At present, billions of tonnes of soil nutrients are not returned to the soil each year through our mismanagement of human and animal waste. For example, instead of benefiting the organisms in the soil, our vast sewage systems are complex, expensive and pollute many of our major rivers, lakes and oceans. Farmers in many areas will have to return to organic fertilizer and abandon petrochemical-based fertilizers and pesticides, if they want to preserve the fertility of their land.

The Tropical Forest in the Philippines

The Global 2000 Report carries data from around the world on the Earth's resources, particularly those which are under threat today. It is very understandable that food, land, water, important minerals and energy should be included. But the inclusion of forests, especially tropical rain forests, might seem strange and unwarranted when compared with air and water. Many people might feel that we cannot live without fresh air, but we can survive without rain forests.

Maybe humans will survive without rain forests but it will be existing, not living. Tropical rain forests are among the richest life systems in the world. They contain millions of plants, animals, insects and birds. In the Philippines alone the forests contain almost 20,000 plant species and many more species of mosses, fungi and algae. The richness of plant life also supports a wide variety of animals and birds. Again, in the Philippines there are over 900 species or subspecies of birds. The best known is the Philippine eagle. This majestic bird – the second largest eagle in the world – is found in Luzon, the Visayas and Mindanao. I will say more about the importance of this bird on pages 36–7.

But the importance of the forests does not end at their boundaries. Forests are important both for the immediate environment and for the Earth as a whole. Tropical forests are intimately bound up with the quality of our air and water; they preserve soil; they moderate climate and affect water distribution. They are one of nature's most abundant nurseries, supplying the raw material for the plants that feed and heal us.

Yet this fragile and irreplaceable life system is being savagely depleted. An area the size of Cuba is being destroyed each year. Obviously this cannot continue indefinitely. Many experts predict that by the year 2020, most tropical forests outside of the Amazon and a small area in West Africa will have been cleared, with disastrous consequences for other life-forms on Earth, especially human beings.

This nightmare of destruction on a world scale has, unfortunately, taken place in the Philippines and especially Mindanao in recent years. The title of a chapter in a recent book, 'Mindanao Wood Industry: A Stripped Land and Uprooted People'[7] – says it all.

Originally, most of the land area of the Philippines – 30 million hectares – was covered with dense, tropical rain forests. Since the 1920s, but particularly after World War II, logging became a major, export-oriented industry. Foreign logging companies and local elites, who often acted as a front for these companies, reaped enormous profits from logging. They tore valleys, hills and mountains apart in order to get the logs to American and Japanese boats waiting in the harbours. Virtually no attention was, or is, paid to understanding this extraordinary life-system, and little care is taken to minimize damage to young trees and other life-forms.

Replanting trees, although a legal requirement for gaining a logging concession, is treated as a joke. A visit to the Security and Exchange Commission reveals why this is so: most of the local entrepreneurs engaged in the logging business are either important politicians or army officers. They know that they can disregard forestry legislation with impunity.

The damage begun by the loggers is further compounded by shifting cultivators. This has been particularly true in Mindanao during the past forty years. Until then, Mindanao had a low population density composed mainly of tribal people, both Muslim and animist. Two factors have sent people from the island of Luzon and the central islands of the Visayas streaming towards Mindanao in recent decades. The first was the growing population; we will see in Part 2 how the population of the Philippines has doubled four times in this century. The second was an unwillingness on the part of the American administration and of successive Filipino governments after independence to face squarely the need for massive land reform programmes on Luzon and in the Visayas. Rather than break up the large, export-oriented plantations and distribute the land to the peasants, the government encouraged thousands of landless peasants to migrate to Mindanao. Within a decade or so, large tracts of the lowland forest and mangrove swamps were cleared or drained. These were often parcelled out to the elite or more recently allowed to fall into the hands of transnational agribusiness corporations. So today's landless peasants follow the loggers into the hills in order to clear some land to till. Within a short period of time – four to five years – the soil is exhausted and eroded, so they move deeper and deeper into the hills, repeating in each place the cycle of destruction.

Very often official publications blame the slash-and-burn agriculture of tribal peoples for the destruction of the forest. It is important to make a distinction here between the slash-and-burn agriculture traditionally practised by tribal peoples, and the slash-and-burn techniques of lowland peasant farmers forced up into the mountains because there is no land for them in the plains. The tribal farmers are sensitive to the environment, according to anthropologists like Conklin who have studied tribal agriculture in Southeast Asia. They argue that this kind of agriculture is sustainable in the long term because the cultivators constantly move their gardens and thus allow the forest to regenerate. These techniques, however, are not sustainable, as the burning is very extensive and continuous cultivation quickly erodes the topsoil. In fact, this kind of agriculture is often based on a misconception about the quality of soil in tropical rain forests. Because of the lush growth of trees and vines, people often think that the soil must be very fertile. In reality, the soil in many tropical rain forests is not very rich. Constant rainfall weathers the soil and the organic matter does not build up in the soil but is quickly recycled back into the vegetation by a variety of insects and fungi. Once the rain forest cover is cleared by logging or burning the trees, the thin layer of soil is exposed and is quickly blown away or eroded. Both in South America and in Southeast Asia, landless peasants who have been elbowed out of prime agricultural land in the lowlands are causing enormous damage to the forests. Yet even here the blame lies more with those who support and encourage plantation, cash-crop agriculture, than with the poor peasants who are trying to eke out a living for themselves and their families on the slopes of the rain forest.

The denuding of forests is proceeding at an alarming rate in the Philippines. In the late 1960s and through the 1970s logging companies and landless peasants destroyed at least 170,000 hectares of forest each year according to NEDA (The National Economic and Development Agency of the Philippines). Recent satellite pictures indicate that the NEDA figures probably underestimate the damage. They now show that less than 30 percent of the country has forest cover. If the present trends continue, all the primary forests will be gone before the year 2000.

The negative effects of logging are numerous. When the forest cover is removed, fragile topsoil, especially on hillsides, is quickly eroded. This in turn silts up river beds, irrigation canals and estuaries, rendering useless expensive irrigation projects and destroying rich agricultural land and fishing grounds. The felling of the forests and the destruction of the watershed leads to severe and widespread flooding during typhoons and monsoons, as there are no trees to absorb the water. A succession of typhoons in the Philippines during August, September and November of 1984 devastated vast tracts of land on the east coast of Mindanao and many islands in the Visayas, especially Cebu and Negros. They are probably a harbinger of worse damage in the years to come.

The day of reckoning has arrived in the Philippines. *The*

Bulletin Today, a national daily, reported from Cebu on 23 July 1984 under the headline, *Central Visayas Imperilled*. The Regional Development Council warned that due to the destruction of forest, and the unwise exploitation of resources, rivers were drying up, massive soil erosion had taken place, marine life was being destroyed and seawater was seeping into groundwater. All of these were signs, according to the report, of impending disaster which could turn the area into a desert early in the next century.

The same message was carried in a Mindanao weekly called *The Misamis Weekly* (18 February 1984). The headline – *The Rape of the Forests* – said that continual logging was turning Central Mindanao into a desert. The National Irrigation Administration (NIA) warns that many of their irrigation projects are drying up as the watershed is destroyed. In the Midsayap-Libungan plain in North Cotabato, the destruction of the watershed has reduced the productivity of 8,000 hectares of prime farmland. In Lanao del Norte only 45 percent of the irrigation system is now effective. The situation is so critical that NIA issued a warning to local authorities that unless the forest destruction is stopped, 'the region's productive land will become barren by the year 2000'.

The picture is bleak and the future looks even grimmer. In the present economic crisis in the Philippines, hopes for an end to illegal logging are slim. Any resource that can yield scarce foreign capital will be exploited in a reckless way. This is the opinion of Rufino T. Magbanua in a report to *The Bulletin Today*, 24 September 1984: due to the 'lax implementation of forestry laws, illegal logging is worsening in Mindanao.' In 1983, 1,023 million cubic metres of logs were exported to Japan from Mindanao. The quota set by the Ministry of National Resources was 600,000 cubic metres, which means that over 400,000 cubic metres was smuggled out of the country. The Aquino government is now trying to halt the destruction of the remaining rain forest by revoking logging permits and encouraging reafforestation.

We have seen that logging is one of the main forces destroying the forest in the Philippines. The demand of First-World countries for hardwood is insatiable. It has increased fifteen-fold since World War II. Japan, for example, has stringent legislation guarding its own forest, yet it is responsible for over half the hardwood imports from developing countries. The bulk of the imports come from Southeast Asia, and high tariffs on finished wood products ensure that the exports are in the form of logs. This effectively precludes the development of a wood processing industry in the source countries. The First-World country has it all its own way: cheap raw material from producer countries with the manufacturing side of the industry concentrated in its hands.

It is hard to visualize that a meal in one's favourite fast-food restaurant damages the tropical forest. Yet it most surely does. The conversion of tropical rain forest to cattle ranches to supply the fast-food hamburger industry of First-World countries is the most wasteful and destructive use of the tropical rain forest. The land is normally cleared through burning the cover. The soil is quickly degraded as erosion is speeded up by the constant pressure of cattle hooves on the fragile soil. When the land becomes exhausted, the ranches move on to repeat the cycle of destruction. The beef thus produced is cheaper, less than half or one-third the cost of beef produced in the US, so it is readily snapped up by the fast-food industries. In this way the cycle of destruction irreversibly destroying the tropical forest can begin with that cheap hamburger.

As we have seen above, the regional and global repercussions of deforestation are catastrophic for agriculture and may induce dramatic climatic changes. One area which is particularly important, and has not received sufficient attention, is the destruction of species on an unprecedented scale. The forest cover is the habitat for up to two million species of plants, insects and animals. Paul and Anne Ehrlich in their book *Extinction* estimate that, given the present rate of destruction, 25 percent of all life-forms on Earth could be extinguished by the first decade of the next century. Extinction on such a scale is not an easy concept to grasp. Because it is so horrendous, it may be something which our conscious collective psyche prefers to ignore, particularly when it arises directly from human technologies. And yet, if we are to understand the magnitude of the changes which are taking place in the biosphere – the most massive change since the dinosaurs died out at the end of the Mesozoic era 60 million years ago – we must confront squarely the terrible slaughter involved in extinction. Thomas Berry in the *Riverdale Papers*[8] insists that extinction is:

> an eternal concept. It is not at all like a killing of individual life forms that can be renewed through normal processes of reproduction. Nor is it simply diminished numbers. Nor is it damage that can somehow be remedied, or for which some substitute can be found. Nor is it something that simply affects our own generation. Nor is it something that can be remedied by some supernatural power. No! it is an absolute and final act for which there is no remedy on earth or in heaven. A species once extinct is gone forever. However many generations succeed us in the coming centuries none of them will ever see a passenger pigeon in flight or any of the other living forms that we extinguish.

Many conservation groups in different countries publish lists of endangered species in their area. The most famous endangered species in the Philippines is the magnificent Philippine eagle. While I was writing this book in April 1985, a very unusual event took place at the Santa Cruz Mission in Lake Sebu, South Cotabato. A young male Philippine eagle was forced down by a group of hornbills over the lake. It became entangled in the nets used in the fish pens on the lake. The bird was captured by a fisherman and brought over to our area. Immediately we sent for personnel of the Philippine Eagle Conservation Program in Davao City so that they could study the bird and determine whether he had been injured and was in need of medication.

A large bamboo aviary was constructed for the 10 days' duration of the eagle's stay at the mission. During that time hundreds of tribal people flocked in to view the bird. Their folklore had many legends about the bird, though few had actually seen a Philippine eagle before as the eagle normally avoids places where its habitat will be disturbed by humans. The older T'boli leaders felt that this bird, having come in such a mysterious way, had a profound message for the people. People who saw the eagle had no problem believing that this must be so. One could not look at this majestic bird, standing three feet high and with a wing span of seven feet, and not feel moved by a sense of beauty and wonder.

The old folks are right, the bird does have a message. What that message is became clearer as I talked at night time with Ronal Krupa, the director of the Philippine Eagle Conservation Program. When the country was almost completely forested, Krupa estimates that there were around 11,000 birds in the whole country. Today the number is down to about 150 pairs. The species is on the verge of extinction, not so much because of hunting and trapping, but principally because of the destruction of the eagle's habitat – the rain forest. The Philippine Eagle Conservation Program is trying to educate people about the plight of this bird. Charles Lindberg, who was associated with setting up the conservation programmes, referred to the eagle as 'the air's noblest flier'. Krupa and his team are also trying to breed the bird in captivity as an eleventh-hour effort to save it from extinction. Krupa points out that apart from the intrinsic value of this species, which is inestimable, this bird is like the miner's canary. If the despoiled environment cannot support the eagle, it will support fewer and fewer species in the future. Dr Dioscoro Rabor, Filipino ornithologist, who first called attention to the peril facing the eagle in 1960, reiterates this. He points out that nine species and subspecies of birds have become extinct in recent years on the island of Cebu alone.

On a world-wide level, the *International Union For The Conservation of Nature & Natural Resources* regularly publishes an updated list of endangered species. The list includes 800 species of higher animals. These include the great whales, the Asian elephants, many different species of cats and a host of birds and animals, mainly from the tropical forests. But this list is only the tip of the iceberg, as it is mainly confined to mammals and birds. By far the most extensive destruction is taking place among plants and insects. Some estimate that one in ten plants is threatened with extinction in the next twenty-five years. It is also predicted that the rate of extinction will increase so that by the year 1990, 10,000 species will be extinguished each year.

The loss to the Earth community of such a diversity of life-forms is enormous. Some authors use the image of rivets in a plane. If a person is flying at a high altitude and sees a single rivet flying off, he may not be unduly worried. If he sees thousands of rivets flying off in all directions, if he is at all normal, he will be terrified. Rivets are flying off the body of life. We do not know what the point of no return might be. We do know, however, that the extinction of a sizeable percentage of life-forms in the biosphere is extremely serious and that as a result the quality of our lives will be much diminished. Although the vast majority of people are hardly aware of it, we are creating a blighted planet, shorn of its natural grandeur, where only rats, cockroaches and other pests will thrive.

Agriculture will also lose precious genetic resources. An article in *Time*, 16 October 1981, entitled 'Tampering with Beans and Genes', draws attention to this. It speaks of the exciting possibilities for food production opened up by research into the genetic structure of plants, particularly those grown in the highly competitive environment of the tropical forest. The diverse and sturdy ecosystem of the tropical forest has, over the aeons, endowed the life-forms there with a high degree of resistance to a variety of disease and pests. Recent advances in genetics make it possible today to transfer these genes to common cereals and other widely used food crops; this in turn reduces the need for the large-scale use of petrochemical fertilizers and pesticides. On a related front, the recent discovery of a strain of perennial corn in the Mexican rain forest could revolutionize corn production by eliminating the need for ploughing and replanting each year. This is good news for the millions who are hungry today. It is also good news for the farmers, as it will help reduce costs. Finally, it is good news for the land. There is only one problem: all of these exciting possibilities, not just for this generation, but for all generations to come, would be terminated forever with the extinctions of the forests.

The loss of so many living forms will be keenly felt in medicine. Drugs derived from the rain forest were at the forefront in combating hypertension, rheumatoid arthritis, Hodgkin's disease and leukemia during the past twenty years. A child suffering from leukemia twenty years ago was almost certainly doomed to die. Today, he or she has a good chance of survival due to a drug derived from *rosy periwinkle*, a plant found in the tropical rain forests of Madagascar.

Some of the effects of the destruction of the forests are seldom alluded to by government planners because they are borne by the tribal people who live in the vicinity of the forest. In the Philippines, the tribal people are on the lowest rung of the political ladder, so their concerns have little political clout. Most government agencies are not geared to respond to their needs. Even those agencies which were set up specifically to help tribal peoples have often destroyed people's environment and culture. So government planners, when they set about evaluating the economic benefits of a logging operation, seldom understand the important place the forest has played in the physical and cultural survival of tribal people.

The T'boli, for example, depend on the forest for their staple food – root crops, a wide variety of edible plants, nuts, fruits and animals. The forest provides their housing needs and firewood to cook their meals. Their medicinal herbs also come from the forest. But the relationship with the forest does not stop there. T'boli art and music is intimately bound up with the forest and dies as the forest is cut down.

The ikat cloth, called *T'nalak*, comes from the forest. So does the beeswax for their brass casting. The timber for many of their musical instruments, both flutes and the two-stringed lute called the *hegelung*, is also found in the forest. Many of the musicians and singers draw inspiration for their songs, music and poetry from the forest. Given this intimate, all-embracing and creative relationship with the forest, one can well imagine what happens when this cycle is broken. Yet the T'boli, or any other tribal group for that matter, are never consulted about, or justly compensated for, the use and depletion of their most precious resources.

The treatment meted out to the Tinggians who live in Abra in Luzon is a case in point. In 1974, ten days after the promulgation of Presidential Decree 410, which was supposed to protect the ancestral lands of tribal peoples, 200,000 hectares of their forest was given to a logging and pulp company called Cellophil Resources Corporation without any consultation with the Tinggians. Cellophil turned a deaf ear to modest requests from tribal leaders not to destroy their fish pens and irrigation canals by floating logs down stream; not to log steep watershed areas and to set aside some communal forests and pasture areas for the tribal people. Representation was made on many occasions to the government by tribal leaders. The government responded by increasing the military presence in the area, which told the people whose side the government was on.

Today, ten years later, the effects of indiscriminate logging are being felt. Cellophil are ready to pull out of the area. The environmental damage which their operation caused is incalculable. The Tinggians are left behind. Much of their once beautiful and bountiful forest is now degraded. Rice production is down. Fishing, a traditional source of protein for the people, has dramatically fallen off because of siltation and landslides, and floods are common. Their very survival as a tribal society is put at risk. Why did Cellophil get the concession in the first place, as it was completely against the interests of the tribal people? A possible answer is that Cellophil is a subsidiary of the Herdis group of companies. The owner, Herminio Disini, is related to Imelda Marcos by marriage and was a golfing partner of Mr Marcos.[9]

History records the extinction of the Mayan civilization after its flourishing for nine hundred years not because of wars, but mainly because of soil erosion resulting from uninterrupted cultivation of corn after the disappearance of the forest. The Carthaginians, Mesopotamians and many others suffered a similar fate; once again, deforestation was a significant factor in the demise of these civilizations. The same phenomenon is at work today. In recent years it is not a coincidence that countries that have experienced extensive deforestation – Bangladesh, Ethiopia, Sudan, India, Pakistan and the Sahel region of Africa – have all suffered crop failures, famine and devastating floods.

Although the tropical rain forest is one of the richest life-systems on Earth, it is poorly understood or appreciated. If the present destruction by loggers, ranchers and slash-and-burn farmers continues unabated, within a generation this vibrant, diverse ecosystem which has dominated the tropics for millions of years will be no more. The life-style of many First World people, unwittingly in many instances, contributes to the destruction. Our new furniture or high meat diet is cutting away at the base of the forest. All future generations will be impoverished. Stringent measures are necessary in

Third-World countries if the destruction is to be halted and reforestation programmes initiated. These will not succeed unless they are accompanied by a major change in consumer demands in First-World countries.

These reflections show how extinction of the rain forests destroys the diversity and fruitfulness of the Earth community. Such destruction weakens the fabric of this community and could, in the not too distant future, bring about a massive collapse within the biosphere. It also impoverishes the human component of the Earth community. As we have seen, our food, water, clothing, shelter and medicine come to us from the Earth community, so any damage to that ultimately affects us all.

Water Pollution

In a talk delivered in Stockholm in 1972 Thor Heyerdahl – a man who has emulated ancient mariners by crossing the Pacific in a raft and the Atlantic in papyrus boats – asked the question, 'What are we doing to the oceans?' He reminded his audience that life began in the oceans and that the oxygen in the atmosphere, on which all respiratory animals are dependent, was produced by the plant plankton in the oceans. If we kill this plankton in the ocean we lose the fish who feed on it, and, more ominously, half the oxygen supply available to human beings and other animals. But many will ask: is it really possible for humans to kill the ocean? Heyerdahl says yes, if we continue to treat it as the Earth's sink. Today we flush almost everything into the ocean and hope that it goes away. This includes pesticides, insecticides, detergents, lead, zinc, copper, cadmium, nickel, heavy metals and petroleum, chemicals and nuclear, industrial, human and animal waste – much of which is non-biodegradable material. We forget that only a fraction of the ocean needs to be polluted to kill all marine life. This is because most life in the ocean is concentrated near the surface and close to the coasts.

All the polluted rivers in the world dump their waste right onto the continental shelf. And the present volume of waste is enormous. In the early 1970s, French rivers carried 18,000

million cubic metres of pollution each year to the sea. The
figures for the Federal Republic of Germany are 9,000 million
cubic metres per year, not counting cooling water which
amounts to 33.6 million cubic metres per day. Each day
50,000 tons of waste are discharged into the Rhine, including
30,000 tons of sodium chloride.

In the Philippines, 362 out of a total of 412 rivers in the
country are polluted to some degree, according to the National
Pollution Control Council. The Pasig river, which flows
through Manila, used to support fresh-water fish. Today it is
biologically 'dead', polluted by 138 industrial firms and
sewage. On the island of Negros, Sugar Centrals pollutes
rivers and the nearby ocean with by-products, especially
molasses. Most destructive of all in the rural areas are the
twenty-four active mines which disgorge more than 100,000
tonnes of tailings daily in rivers and coastal water.

Besides the rivers and pipelines carrying poisons into the
seas, noxious fumes from industries, homes and automobiles
also end up in the seas. In the United States alone 142 million
tons of air-borne pollution end up every year in the oceans. Oil
pollution is also causing grave concern to ecologists. It only
made headlines when a supertanker like the *Torrey Canyon*
discharged 100,000 tonnes of crude oil into the English
Channel. What the media fail to report is that much more than
100,000 tonnes of oil is intentionally discharged each year
from the world's navies and merchant fleets. Add to this the
routine washing of oil tankers, and one can see why Heyerdahl
saw solidified blobs of oil strung right across the ocean during
the crossing of the Atlantic in his papyrus boat, the *RA*. The
larger oil clots were often covered with barnacles or marine
worms, and thus became an attractive bait for fish. When
human beings eat the fish the pollution finds its way back into
human tissue.

I have already drawn attention to the problems associated
with the acid rain and the pollution of fresh-water rivers and
lakes from pesticides and agricultural run-off. The condition
of water and lack of access to fresh water is becoming so
serious in many areas of the world that the *Rocky Mountain
Institute* in Colorado predicts that water will replace energy as
the most prominent resources issue in the 1990s. In the United

States, irrigation is undermining ancient groundwater reservoirs. Ogallala Aquifer beneath the six Plains states is being drawn down by 4 to 10 feet each year. The replacement rate is about a quarter-inch per year. Obviously this cannot continue indefinitely.

The sea is also an important source of food for many people, but here again human demands are seriously depleting fish stocks. Between 1950 and 1970 the annual increase in fishery catches was seven percent. The high point was reached in 1975, when 70 million tonnes of fish were taken from the seas. In the process, stocks of herring, mackerel and anchovy, to mention just three, were seriously depleted so that there has been significant decrease in our intake from the sea since then. The major culprits are the large fishing fleets from the USSR and Japan which scoop everything up from the oceans and process the fish on the high seas. Since the catches of conventional fish are down, some of these fleets are turning their attention to the krill in the Antarctic. While there is an enormous quantity of krill in the sea, a serious depletion of stocks could have catastrophic consequences for other species in the area such as whales, seals and penguins which feed on the krill.

In recent years, two other extremely productive marine ecosystems in the Philippines—coral reefs and mangroves—have also been threatened. As an archipelago with more than 7,000 islands, the Philippines is richly endowed with numerous varieties of coral species on extensive reefs covering an estimated 44,000 square kilometres. The coral reefs are composed of many living animals and skeletons of thousands of dead corals. They are the home of an incredible variety of marine life – fish, crabs, molluscs and seaweed – and are nature's nursery for much of our aquatic life. They also act as a barrier, protecting the coast line from the pounding of tropical storms. For the diver the brilliant colours and the varied shapes of the corals themselves are a world of beauty and enchantment not found elsewhere on Earth.

Sad to say, this unique Philippines ecosystem is dying. An extensive survey of coral reefs carried out jointly by the University of the Philippines' Marine Science Center and Silliman University in Dumaguete City found that only five percent of the corals surveyed were in excellent shape. Almost fifty percent are seriously damaged. A number of factors are working together to destroy the corals. The most important seems to be siltation.

Corals are very delicate creatures and the murky waters carried down from denuded hillsides kill the coral polyps or seriously retard their growth. This cycle of destruction once again illustrates the interconnectedness of natural systems. Other factors involved in the demise of coral reefs are destructive fishing techniques such as using dynamite, and the export of corals to the United States, Australia, Europe and Japan. A presidential decree in 1977 prohibited the exportation of corals. The ban is not strictly enforced. The increasing demand for coral to decorate house aquaria in First World countries means that large quantities of corals are still being smuggled out of the country. Unless these practices are discontinued there will be few coral reefs left in the country in twenty years time. The death of coral reefs will mean a serious decline in fish, since most species of fish feed in coastal ecosystems. For Filipinos whose staple diet is composed of fish, rice and vegetables, this will mean more malnutrition and death.

Mangroves are located on tidal flats and along the coastlines in a tropical environment. They are characterized by poor soil aeration and high salinity, conditions which preclude the growth of many kinds of plant life. Nevertheless these conditions are ideal for many species. Like the coral reefs, mangroves are the breeding and feeding grounds for a variety of fish. Mangroves are also the home for many species of wildlife, birds, reptiles, amphibians and insects. They act as a sort of filtering system for industrial pollution and eroded soil. Wood from the mangroves is particularly hard and durable so it has many commercial uses apart from providing building material for nearby residents.

Unfortunately these beneficial services of the mangroves are not recognized by planners or the public at large. For this reason mangroves have probably suffered the worst fate of any ecosystem in the Philippines. In 1920 the extent of mangroves in the Philippines was estimated at around 500,000 hectares. Today the figure is less than 150,000 hectares. Some of the sources of pressure have already been mentioned – pesticide run-offs, mine tailings and the clearing of land for agricultural and commercial purposes. Other factors include the conversion of mangroves to commercial fishponds and the construction of luxury resorts. Whatever the cause, the chain reaction will be dearly felt by many Filipinos. Wiping out the mangroves means less nutrients for algae which in turn means less food for the fish. Less fish for the people means more hunger.

The above is a bird's-eye view of what is happening to our air, sunlight, soil, forests, various life-forms and water – the natural life-system of our Earth. In an extensive way the damage is the fruit of our modern industrial, commercial culture which is not establishing any sustainable relationship with the natural world. This comes as a shock to us. We feel that our technologies, which give us our roads, houses, modern diet, factories, space shuttle and computers, are becoming more and more sophisticated. Individual items might decay but our technologies have the stamp of permanence about them. The message of the ecological movement and of this book is that there is another, more accurate story. Our foul air, polluted waters and oceans, shrinking croplands, creeping deserts and extinguished species tell the true story. They bear the hidden costs of our increasingly powerful technologies, costs which are often left out of the economists' calculations. The Earth's ledger, which in the final analysis is the only real one, tells us that the Earth is finite and vulnerable, and that natural systems will be seriously depleted and possibly collapse unless human beings begin to shape their lives in the light of this reality of ecological accounting.

Diminishing our Humanity

The impoverishment which flows from this destruction goes far beyond our physical needs. We also diminish our own humanity when we destroy our environment because we are integral with the life community. Our senses of wonder, beauty and joy come from the profusion of colour, pattern and music in the world around us. Our imagination is stimulated by the wonderful diversity in our world. Human liturgies, music, art, poetry and dance give conscious expression to the rhythms and melodies of the birds, the wind in the trees and running water in the rivers. The creation symphonies of the great composers do not arise simply from their individual genius but are inspired by the natural world. This music celebrates the wonders of the Earth.

Thomas Berry[10] points out that if we were born on the Moon and lived all our lives there, our imagination would reflect the desolation of the lunar landscape. Our sensitivity would also be dull; lacking warmth, colour and nuance. Our language too would be extremely restricted, since there would be so few things to name. So the more lunar-like we make the planet the more we are destroying ourselves. The fact that many people do not appreciate this is itself a tragedy. It is, however, a daily experience of teachers and social workers who are close to children living in squalid, run-down slums. People who are constantly surrounded by waste-lands and ruins, with no access to beauty, suffer serious retardation in their emotional and spiritual lives.

The great Rhineland mystic, Meister Eckhart, calls attention to the revelatory dimension of every creature when he insists that 'every creature is a word of God and a book about God'.[11] St Thomas Aquinas has much the same thing in mind in the *Summa*, Part 1, Question 47, Article 1.[12] He argues that God created a magnificent variety of creatures so that his goodness might be communicted to them and reflected by them.

> Hence we must say that the distinction and multitude of things comes from the intention of the first agent, who is God. For He brought things into being in order that His goodness might *be communicated to creatures and be represented by them; and because His goodness could not be adequately represented by one creature alone. He produced many and diverse creatures so that, what was wanting to one in the manifestation of the Divine goodness, might be supplied by another. For goodness, which in God is simple and uniform, in creatures is manifold and divided; and hence the whole universe together participates in the divine goodness*

more perfectly and represents it better than any single creature whatever. (Italics mine)

Our profound and wonderful sense of the Divine comes to a great extent from the beauty and diversity of the natural world. The Psalmist uses the image of the cedars of Lebanon, while the book of Exodus compares God's love and care for the People of Israel to that of the eagle who bears her young on her wings (Ex. 19:4). So when we extinguish species we destroy forever the possibilities that those species had for representing in a unique way the mystery of God.

Some people will, however, argue that extinction should not cause us too much worry because the life community is a vital, living reality and some species are always dying out while others are evolving. While it is true that species die out in their natural habitat, the rate at which this takes place naturally is very limited, particularly in the more recent Earth history of the Cenozoic or Tertiary period. During this time, life-forms have come and gone but over all, the planet has been enriched. Our generation, on the other hand, is extinguishing life-forms in a very unproductive manner. There is no cumulative enrichment; instead we are beginning to sterilize the planet and make it less hospitable for living organisms.

For the first time in the history of the Earth, modern industrial society is a world-wide phenomenon, its extractive tentacles reaching every corner of the globe. Since I live and work in the Philippines I have quoted many examples to show what is happening here. In this archipelago, with its abundance of natural resources, its diversified and sturdy ecosystem, I am watching the natural world being torn apart, poisoned, raped. Within the past thirty years or so, this once healthy environment has taken enormous punishment. Almost every ecosystem is now seriously impaired.

3

IRELAND DESPOILED

Ecology is about relationships of interdependence on this small planet Earth. Our air, water, sunlight, soil and living forms are part of a global commons. Many of the examples quoted illustrate how life-forms thousands of miles away are affected by pollution in a distant part of the world. The wind and air currents blow free. Acid rain, which originates in the US, England and the Ruhr Valley in Germany, destroys lakes and woodlands in Canada and Scandinavia. The same is true of polluted water. In reality there is no such thing as territorial waters. The waters from Irish rivers that run into the Atlantic today are carried elsewhere within a day by ocean currents. The loss of genetic diversity in the Philippines impoverishes all the citizens of the Earth, because plants have fed and cured human beings since we emerged on Earth.

So people in Ireland or other western countries cannot just shrug their shoulders and sigh: 'Too bad for the Filipinos; it does not really hurt me. Since there is little I can do, it is better to forget about it.' True, the brunt of the damage will, unfortunately, be borne by present and future generations of Filipinos. But it should also worry everyone. We are partly responsible for the damage, since living standards in First-World countries create the demand for Third-World timber and natural resources. People in the First–World and, especially, their children will eventually also be called on to pay for the wastefulness of today. Damage to any one of the global commons quickly spreads elsewhere. This is the *raison d'être* for the ecological slogan: 'Think globally – act locally now'.

But what of the local situation in Ireland? Surely there is no cause for alarm? The Irish, both at home and overseas, have celebrated the beauty of the country. Their ballads tell of 'Four Green Fields', 'Forty Shades of Green', 'The Green of Antrim'. The tourist brochures urge Americans and Europeans to fish from the pollution-free, if not always sunny, beaches!

It is good to begin by putting this 'Emerald Isle' image of Ireland, with which we are all so familiar, into perspective. It probably comes as a surprise to realize that a countryside of grasslands, bogs and cultivated fields is only of recent origin. As the ice of the last ice-age receded, vegetation once again quickly covered the countryside. Ten thousand years ago, a mere instant on the geological clock, Ireland had a temperate forest cover. Oak and elm grew on the better soil, alder in wet areas and pine on the poor soil. This forest cover was only broken by mountains and wetlands. The first neolithic farmers to arrive in Ireland began cutting the forest about five thousand years ago. Naturally, the progress was slow at first, but as the tools improved and the need for pasture lands and timber, at home and abroad, increased, more trees fell under the axe. Apart from a few isolated areas all the original forest was cut by the beginning of World War I.

The felling of the forest did not pass unmourned. The impoverishment and desolation of the countryside and the destruction of wild-life is captured in the poignant lament by a Munster poet in the eighteenth century: 'Cad a dheanfaimid feasta gan adhmad, tá deire na gcoitle are lár? (What shall we do without timber, all the woods are cut?)' It is important not to let nostalgia blind us to the fact that in Ireland neither the native Irish, nor the colonizers, have lived lightly on the Earth. Nevertheless, the damage to date may well pale by comparison with what is at present taking place, unless a new attitude of caring for creation emerges among the people. It is sobering to note that most of the natural habitats to survive undamaged have done so either because they were not considered profitable to exploit, or because they were relatively inaccessible until recent times.

What are some of the disturbing patterns that have emerged in recent years that should be causing major concern to civic,

religious and political leaders? Since I have spent the greater
part of the past sixteen years in the Philippines I did not have
immediate access to detailed reports on the recent damage to
ecosystems in Ireland. Most of the examples I quote are taken
from newspapers and journals. They point towards an
increasingly destructive trend. In 1985 as this book was being
completed, An Foras Forbartha published a book called *The
State of the Environment*.[1] This is the first comprehensive
report on the state of the Irish environment and it too
concludes that with the increase in urban and rural pollution
there is cause for concern.

Water Pollution

In *The Sunday Tribune*, 8 August 1982, a feature article by
Donal Musgrave states that 'Lough Derg has become a giant
receptacle for human waste, industrial effluent, silage runoffs
and turf mould from Midland bogs'. The article attempts to
raise the alarm about what is happening to the second largest
lake in Ireland. It concludes that unless the present levels of
pollution are drastically reduced, Lough Derg will die within
the next twenty to thirty years. This would be a catastrophe
for the entire country but particularly for the counties of
North Tipperary, East Clare and East Galway. Many of the
same factors, especially sewage, which induce a proliferation
of algae, causing eutrophication, are also worrying scientists at
the New University of Ulster who are monitoring Lough
Neagh and attempting to devise schemes to draw off the
dangerous phosphates. One of the scientists involved in this
programme concluded an interview with the BBC early in
1985 with the ominous warning that unless they succeed in
treating the water coming into the lake, 'you can say goodbye
to Lough Neagh'. Imagine what that would mean for the
extensive fishery industry and for the birds, animals and
people who live in the area.

The Sunday Tribune returned to the same theme of water
pollution on 22 August 1982. This time it included data on
the pollution of the coastal waters from industrial effluent and
untreated sewage. Dr David Cabot, head of the conservation
and research department at An Foras Forbartha, maintained

that the EEC policy on pollution and environmental protection is simply ignored. The article also calls attention to the marked increase in agricultural pollution in recent years. It points out that there has been a hundred percent increase in nitrate levels in Irish rivers and streams during the past five years. Increased nitrate levels are known to cause birth defects and still births in both the animal and human population. A further prediction from Dr Cabot, 'I believe that many of our lakes could die before the end of the century', should make people sit up and take note.

During the past few years, public water supplies in a number of areas have been contaminated by agricultural waste. I experienced one such incident in my home town, Nenagh, on New Year's Eve, 1982. The local weekly *The Guardian*, 8 January 1983, described the incident with bold headlines, 'Five Million Gallons of Water Contaminated'. The report raised a number of extremely serious and very worrying questions. The chief Sanitary Service Engineer, Mr John O'Flynn, said that 'it was impossible to establish or trace the pollution'. This inability on the part of public authorities to trace a major source of pollution is not a very comforting thought for the residents, particularly if the substance leaked the next time is more toxic.

There was also a serious delay in alerting the public to what had taken place through the national broadcasting and television service. The report in *The Guardian* quotes Mr O'Flynn as saying that he received notice of the leak on Thursday night at 7.30. However, RTE (Radio Telefís Eireann) did not carry the news item until 6.30 pm on Friday. Other public officials played down the incident. The engineer, Mr Seamus Malone, is quoted as saying 'this type of pollution happens once in a half-century; he did not want to overrate the possibility of it happening again'. Luckily he did not have to eat his words. *The Guardian*, 6 July 1985, carried a news item that another pollution threat to the reservoir was averted by swift action on the part of the County Council's maintenance staff. It does not augur too well for the future if public officials take such a cavalier attitude to what could have been a major disaster. One fears that it will take a serious tragedy to awaken public consciousness to very real dangers.

A worrying feature of almost all public officials' response to pollution dangers, which we will see below in relation to nuclear waste, is that they tend to play down the risks involved even when they know that they are serious. The end result today is that the public simply do not believe the reports of many government monitoring bodies.

Water is once again the subject of an article in *The Irish Times*, 27 September 1982. Mr Owen, of the National Board of Science and Technology, complained that domestic and industrial waste discharged into Irish estuaries and coastal waters was increasing at the alarming rate of ten percent per annum. In the same vein, Paddy Woodworth in *The Irish Times*, 20 July 1984, looks at what is happening along a section of the east coast of Ireland in an article entitled 'Dublin Bay, Dump For a City's Rubbish?' He began by noting that many 'euphemisms abound for the mass of raw sewage and associated hygienic products which litter the surface and beaches of Dublin Bay'.

While everyone admits that there has been a phenomenal increase in pollution in recent years, experts seem to differ on whether it constitutes a serious health hazard. Dr Peter Smith, of the Department of Microbiology in University College, Galway, on the one hand, would not allow his children to swim at Dollymount, near Dublin. Dr Fergus Hill, the analyst for Dublin Corporation, has stated categorically that 'there is no satisfactory evidence linking communicable diseases with the degree of sewage contaminating bathing water'. One cannot help wondering whether he would allow his children to swim in contaminated waters. Shane Grey, the public relations officer for the Irish Underwater Council, thinks otherwise. His four sons, who have spent much of their summer vacation swimming in the area, have contracted gastro-enteritis and hepatitis. He draws little comfort from the debate among academics when his nose, eyes and mouth – if he happens to swallow some of the water – tell him something is seriously wrong.

Nuclear Waste

In the late 1982 and early 1983 letters to the daily papers and statements from public figures began to express their concern about the long-term effects of dumping large quantities of radioactive waste 400 miles south of the Irish coast in the Atlantic. The governments that carry out the dumping insist that the containers are leak-proof and, therefore, do not pose short- or long-term health hazards. Most people today are sceptical about such assurances. If the dangers are minimal, why not bury the waste in the country which produced the pollution in the first place? A report to President Reagan and Congress by the National Advisory Committee on Oceans and the Atmosphere in July 1984, while recommending that the US end a moratorium on ocean dumping, concedes that the 'track record of the experts in managing the radioactive waste problem in the past – and in keeping the public properly informed – does not instill confidence in their present management scheme' (*The Irish Times*, 23 July 1984).

The indestructability of the so-called special containers is also in question. Similar containers dropped into the shallower waters of the Irish Sea and English Channel have been moved around and cracked open by currents on the bottom of the sea. The earthquake in the Irish Sea, in what is normally an earthquake-free zone, sent an added chill down the spine of many environmentalists, according to Willie Kealy and Tom Shell in 'Quake Raises Nuclear Waste Fear', in *The Sunday Independent*, 22 July 1984.

Des Hickey in *The Sunday Independent*, 9 January 1983, turns his attention to another kind of nuclear contamination, this time in the Irish Sea. He asks: 'Must the Irish Sea be an atomic dump?' He was complaining about the radioactive effluent released into the Irish Sea from the Windscale (now Sellafield) plant in northern England. This plant is described by some scientists are the 'dirtiest nuclear plant in the world'. Consequently, according to Dr Peter Michell of the Department of Physics, University College Dublin, the Irish Sea holds an unenviable record. It is now the most radioactive sea in the world.

Another article, by Declan Kennedy in *The Irish Times*, 31 January 1983, decries this out-of-sight, out-of-mind approach to something with as long-term and lethal effects as radioactive material. Even a rudimentary knowledge of the mechanisms of the food chain warns us that substances absorbed by marine organisms end up in human tissue. Unless this form of pollution is severely curtailed we will see in the decades ahead a rise in still births, genetic mutations, and diseases such as cancer.

In 1984 the spotlight of controversy focused on Sellafield in Cumbria, and on Dundalk, a town on the other side of the Irish Sea. The issue was the effects of dumping so-called low-level nuclear waste at sea. An Independent Television programme in the area linked the high incidence of leukemia in local children to the radioactive discharge from Sellafield. An official British Government inquiry in July 1984 confirmed the high incidence of leukemia, but doubted whether radioactivity was the cause. Ecological organizations, like Greenpeace, in both Britain and Ireland, labelled the report a whitewash and called for an end to radioactive discharges from the plant.

The Irish Times, 24 July 1984, reported that Dr Nicholas Napier, whose practice covers 2,500 patients in the Strangford Ardglass area, registered two deaths from acute leukemia within a six-month period in 1980. Dr Napier said that he 'was very concerned about the effects of the dumping of radioactive materials in the Irish Sea'. That same day Mr Patten, from the Northern Ireland Office responsible for health, repeated his Department's assurance that the plant posed no dangers for the people of County Down. Such denials are meeting growing scepticism.

The same edition of *The Irish Times* carried a report on a study being conducted by two Irish scientists, Dr Patricia Sheehan and Dr Irene Hillary, on the possible links between an accidental discharge of radioactivity at Windscale in 1957 and the unusually high incidence of Down's Syndrome babies born to women who were schoolgirls in Dundalk at the time. Preliminary studies showed that six girls out of a class of eleven have since given birth to babies affected by Down's Syndrome. At first it was thought that a virus associated with an outbreak of the Asian 'flu in the area or, at least, the interaction between the virus and the raised radioactive levels might have been responsible. Now the *Irish Times* journalist, Dick Grogan, reports the researchers are saying that 'the thrust of the hypothesis has swung towards a purely radioactivity-induced effect'.

Land Pollution

There are two main sources of pollution affecting agricultural land. The first stems from the industrial and chemical methods of farming, which in recent decades have become such a predominant feature of Irish agriculture. Even the Irish manager of a world-wide chemical producer, Ciba Geigy, complained about the lack of legislation governing the chemicals now used in Irish agriculture. *The Irish Times*, 15 December 1984, quotes him as saying that 'the absence of legislation to ensure that chemicals were of a standard which could protect the interests of the consumers and public in general, was disastrous'. These chemicals are finding their way into rivers, lakes and eventually the sea.

Land pollution from industrial sources is also on the increase. Gerard O'Dwyer, in *The Sunday Tribune*, 1 July 1984, discusses the dangers to animal and human health caused by the dust from the former Mogul mines at Silvermines, County Tipperary. The dust in the area is coming from a 'tailings lake', which contains numerous mineral washings and chemicals, including cyanide. As the lake dries up the dust is blown on to nearby pastures. A number of cattle in the vicinity have died of lead poisoning. Further south in County Tipperary, a local farmer is locked in a legal battle with a multinational chemical firm. According to the farmer, more than seventy cattle have died on his farm during the past three years. While the local County Council have exonerated the company from blame, the farmer is so certain that chemicals from the plant are destroying his farm that he has begun legal action in the High Court.

Refuse dumps are also a source of land pollution in Ireland. Ron Elsdon, in his book *Bent World*,[2] describes the throw-away society which is creating mountains of rubbish. A disturbing factor about the rubbish is that much of it is non-biodegradable. Elsdon estimates that an Irish rural family amasses 30 pounds of rubbish each week while their city cousins bring the scale up to 50 pounds. Aside from the fact that some of the waste is toxic, the accumulating rubbish is a blight on the Irish countryside.

Finally, the extinction of species, which we treated so extensively in Chapter 2, is often thought of as affecting exclusively Third-World countries lying in the tropical region. Unfortunately it also affects countries in the temperate zone. The economics of agriculture in recent decades, which involves shipping food from one corner of the Earth to another, has put enormous pressure on small farms. In England, for example, this economic pressure to establish larger, so-called more productive, farms is responsible for the destruction of 3,200 kilometres of hedgerows and 75,000 hectares of heathlands. The extensive clearing is endangering close to 300 plant species. Undoubtedly the more modern technical farming adopted in recent decades is putting pressure on a variety of species in Ireland. *The State of the Environment* estimates that increased mechanization in agriculture in Ireland has caused a loss of 2 kilometres of hedge per square kilometre since 1936. Most of the loss has occurred since 1973.[3] Fifty-two species of flora, eighteen bird species, one amphibian and three mammals are considered endangered species in Ireland and are thus protected by the Wildlife Act, 1976.[4] The Irish Wildlife Association is particularly perturbed about the wholesale clearing of boglands. They feel that extensive tracts of this unique ecosystem should be left untouched.

Air Pollution

Air pollution is a health hazard in Dublin. According to Pat Brennan in *The Irish Press*, 27 November 1984, Dublin is now one of the unhealthiest places in Europe to live in. The article is entitled, 'When The Air You Breathe Can Kill'. David Byrne, the Assistant City Manager, points out that the poor air standards have come from 'the increase in burning solid fuel for domestic heat'. It is somewhat ironic that the high level of pollution in recent years is due to government-assisted grants to install solid fuel burners after the oil crisis in 1973. The report indicates that neither the Department of Energy nor of the Environment have yet devised plans to deal with the problem. David Byrne suggests that the solution lies with natural gas. While that may be true in the short term, natural gas will not last forever. Some other solution will have to be found. One indicator of the poor quality of the air in Dublin, Cork and Limerick is that few lichens grow on the trees in the centre of the cities. Like the Philippine Eagle, here we have an example of another member of the Earth community, even if perhaps a lowly one, telling us that we are endangering everything including ourselves.

Food

Fintan O'Toole in the *Journal Technology-Ireland*, January 1984, explodes some myths about the wholesomeness of Irish meat and dairy products. Until recently, Irish farmers enjoyed almost unrestricted access to antibiotics, and thus the levels of antibiotic residue have reached serious proportions in meat and dairy products. O'Toole quotes figures released by the Department of Agriculture for the first half of October 1982. They show that 18.7 percent of the Irish sample contain antibiotic residue, against 0.1 percent for Britain and the rest of Europe. The report calls attention to the double standards being used by producers for the local and export markets. Products for export are stringently tested, while those for the local market are not. Fergus Pyle returns to this theme in *The Irish Times*, 31 July 1984, in a report entitled 'Risk Areas For Meat Eaters'. Those in the meat business have a fund of stories on how antibiotics are used as 'growth stimulants, of drug companies pushing their products, of dishonest farmers selling milk to cooperatives from cows stuffed with drugs to combat mastitis'. A Government's Food Advisory Committee report published early in 1984 is aware of the problem and agrees that the risks to the consumer are real. They include hypersensitivity reactions in people with allergies and the development of pathogenic micro-organisms resistant to certain antibiotics.

Much of the material I have quoted from the Press is now available in a single volume entitled *Promises and Performance*.[5] This book is a collection of the papers presented at an environmental conference held in University College Dublin in April 1984. The book analyses environmental issues in Ireland. It looks at government policies and the implementation of these policies at different levels. Many of the

conclusions emerging from the data indict successive governments which have pandered to vested interests instead of
providing comprehensive environmental protection for all
citizens. There is also a call for every citizen to be concerned
about the environment so that a new national consensus can
emerge. This needs to be inculcated in a variety of ways: by
formal and informal educational programmes in the home, the
school and the Churches. Economic planners and farmers
need to initiate a new approach to agriculture which respects
the soil and natural cycles. A new sense of responsibility needs
to emerge among public officials which will ensure that they
put the health of the land and people ahead of the short-term
economic and electoral advantages which highly pollutant
industries hold out to governments. Finally, stringent
legislation is needed to uphold this new determination to
protect the health, beauty and long-term bountifulness of the
country before it is too late. If drastic changes do not take
place in public awareness, the next decade will see a serious
deterioration in an already threatened environment.

A Europe-wide survey carried out in 1985 on the importance of the environment in relation to economic growth
bears this out. Sixty percent of Europeans consulted
considered environmental protection to be more important
than increased economic growth. Only a dismal twenty-nine
percent of the Irish sample shared this concern. It seems that
Irish leaders are not leading the people in encouraging change.

The question arises: From where is the new consciousness
going to emerge, since there are few signs of it in Ireland at
that moment? Despite the fact that hardly a week passes by
without some news item on pollution, public figures,
including Church leaders in the major denominations, have
been slow to speak out on the destruction of the Earth. The
Irish Council of Churches and the Catholic Church did
publish a slim volume called *Environmental Problems in
Ireland*.[6] This book lists environmental research in both parts
of Ireland, a short environmental ethic and a number of
recommendations directed at the Church and society at large.
Like many other excellent books, it does not seem to have
achieved much. For one thing, it is not readily available in the
Churches or regular bookstores. While poverty and related

social justice issues have received an airing in pulpits in recent years, I would wager that the moral and spiritual dimensions of environmental degradation have not figured prominently in Sunday sermons, or moral exhortations from Church leaders. Fortunately, respect and love for the Earth, and a challenge to experience God in the world of nature, does figure prominently in some of the catechetical material used in the schools today.

One can only hope and pray that this concern will become more widespread in the Church before it is too late. After all, what is the value of a little extra money if the fertility of the land is impaired, rivers are contaminated with toxic substances, and numerous bird and animal species lost forever? Why sing about working for the goal of national political unity when, through our present negligence and carelessness, we bequeathe a grimy, dirty and run-down environment to our children? We will have begun to damage beyond repair the natural world, stunt the possibilities for human growth and creativity afforded by a beautiful country and impair our ability to meet and experience God in the world around us. In a real and irreversible way we will have begun to close down the life-systems of the natural world in Ireland.

4

THE DEATH OF AN OLD COSMOGRAPHY

My concern thus far has been to show that in the last two centuries, and increasingly in recent decades, human demands have outstripped the ability of biological systems to renew themselves. I have endeavoured to show that on a global scale and in particular bio-regions like the Philippines and Ireland, humans are in a very significant way altering the structure of the planet. Massive engineering projects – dams, road, irrigation canals, new towns, suburbs and shopping malls – are altering the topography of the Earth. Chemicals in industry and agriculture are polluting the air, water and soil. The denudation of tropical forests is destroying the habitat for thousands of living forms. Mining and other extractive industries are rapidly depleting many scarce energy and mineral resources. This is all happening at an increasing rate. It seems that in our frenzy to process everything, human beings have forgotten how long it took for the Earth to evolve such extraordinary natural resources and such a diverse, interdependent community of living forms which are our companions in the air, swimming through the waters, moving on the land and beneath the soil itself.

Much of our trouble has come from our enchantment with technology. The more sophisticated technology becomes, the more it tends to place humans outside the community of the natural world, so that we feel no real affinity for the Earth and no real sense of loss when it is being seriously scarred and impaired. While it would be foolish to deny the benefits that a certain segment of human beings have reaped from modern technology in terms of better health and long life span, much of the gains may yet prove short-lived if, in the process of achieving them, we destroy the Earth. It seems that our situation today is similar to that of a man who is so preoccupied with his need for firewood and is so impressed with the power-saw in his hand that instead of just cutting a branch, he is sawing down a tree which is tilted in his direction. Unless he wakes up soon to what he is doing, the tree will come crashing down on him. All that will be needed then are a few planks for a coffin!

Why, one might ask, is the human community so short-sighted? Why does it appear to be marching full speed down a road leading to a sickened and rundown planet? Why have the various professions, especially religious leaders, failed to call people's attention to the massive challenges facing the Earth? In a pamphlet called *The New Story*,[1] Fr Thomas Berry argues that our modern malaise and misdirection is in large measure due to the fact that modern western people have lost a meaningful sense of identity. We have no comprehensive *myth or story* to account for the emergence of the world and our place and role in the world. In this sense, we are much poorer than most other societies, ancient or modern. The Greeks had the *Iliad* and *Odyssey*. The world of Hindu India has the *Ramayana* and the *Mahabharata*. In ancient Ireland the bards told the great epic stories like the *Táin*. The Buddhist world has the stories of the Buddha. The T'boli have their epic called *Tudbulul*. All of these stories give human existence a meaning and a place. They enshrine and celebrate the values which are highly prized in the particular society. Most important of all, they stir people to work for the goals of that society. Modern western people, on the other hand, have no such comprehensive story to guide them, particularly, in relating to the natural world. Whatever moral or religious stories we have ignore the Earth, and so we relate to the Earth, as is clear from Chapter 2, in an inadequate, often useless and very destructive way.

The western European world was not always so impoverished, according to Fr Berry. Until the late Middle Ages there was a cosmology based mainly on the Genesis account of creation, interpreted through the framework of neo-Platonism or Aristotelianism. The foundations of the legal and political world and the arts that celebrated natural and human beauty rested on this cosmology. Theological reflection, including Thomas Aquinas's *Summa Theologiae,* was anchored in this perspective.

The coherence and universal acceptance of this story began to diminish in the fifteenth and sixteenth centuries. It would be foolish to blame this on one single event, but it does seem that the Black Death (1347–9) played a decisive role. This plague had a traumatic effect on Europeans in the fourteenth and fifteenth centuries. The disease seemed to come from nowhere, and in many places – like Florence and Venice – it killed half the population in a few weeks. Clerical sermons at the time interpreted the plague as Divine punishment for a wicked generation. For those who felt that generation was no worse than previous ones this interpretation raised serious questions about the Christian faith. It seemed to fly in the face of a belief in a benign God who had created and ordered a just world.[2]

By the beginning of the sixteenth century, this uneasiness with the adequacy of the traditional story of the cosmos had developed into a divorce between those who still maintained that the Earth was the centre of everything and those, like Copernicus, who argued that the Earth spun on its own axis and also moved around a stationary sun. While this new Copernican theory opened up the immense universe for observation, and gave a more adequate explanation for the movement of heavenly bodies, it came as a profound shock to many people. The dethronement of the Earth from the centre of creation was seen as a challenge both to Ptolemaic astronomy and, more important still, to orthodox theology.

Old stories and cosmologies do not die easily. Ecclesiastical authorities tried to re-establish the old myth with the trial and condemnation of Galileo in 1633, but the damage had already been done. The trial was deeply resented by the scientific community. It confirmed its worst suspicions that ecclesiastical authorities would rigidly oppose the development of the new sciences. From this time, science and religion tended to follow separate, often mutually hostile paths, in the western world. Religious thinkers withdrew their attention from wider cosmic, earthly, and even cultural concerns and began to concentrate almost exclusively on the uniqueness of the Christian story. Consequently the theology of creation was generally ignored and almost all theological enquiry was confined to the process of redemption and salvation, the personality of Jesus, the interior spiritual disciplines needed to guide the individual soul along the path of salvation, and the internal constitution and juridical status of the ecclesial community.

The Protestant reformation had split the Western Church by the mid-sixteenth century. Much of the Protestant tradition tended to reject the traditional natural theology of the Scholastics. They insisted on the primacy of salvation and the order of grace.

It is important to note here that my discussion of the Christian experience and response to the Enlightenment and the scientific revolutions which occured from the sixteenth to the twentieth centuries is confined to the Catholic tradition, mainly because as a member of that Church I am better acquainted with its traditions.

While much of what I say applies also to the Protestant tradition in Europe and North America, quite a number of Protestants, particularly those of the liberal tradition, entered into a dialogue with the Enlightenment and emerging scientific disciplines of the time. Catholics and many evangelical Protestants saw this as a sell-out and mounted a constant polemic against such tendencies. They pointed out that the liberal Protestant tradition was swamped by the new knowledge and often seduced into abandoning traditional Christian teaching. This resulted in the broad spectrum of Catholic scholarship and much of evangelical Protestantism shying away from any attempt, such as Aquinas had made in his day, to ground the Christian faith on the emerging cosmological insights.

It is also important to remember that during the following centuries much of the most creative energy in the Christian churches was spent on internecine struggle and rivalry. This left little time for Christian thinkers to understand and interpret the larger cultural and historical movements associated with the Renaissance and the colonial expansion in the Americas, Africa, Asia and Oceania. It also blinded

religious thinkers to what was happening in the scientific
community in Europe and thus prevented them from giving
religious significance to the new cosmic, planetary, geological
and biological discoveries which were then emerging.

Scientists, however, continued to explore the dynamics of
the Earth and living forms. During the eighteenth and
nineteenth centuries geologists, biologists and natural historians began to explore intensely the natural world, both in
Europe and in the New World. The Scottish geologist, James
Hutton (1726–79), began by asking the question: How was the
Earth formed? Rather than simply accepting the Genesis
account as a scientific description for the origins of the Earth,
he maintained that the natural processes now at work –
flowing rivers, rain, tidal action, volcanoes and earthquakes –
have been operating more or less in a similar fashion right
through the long sequence of geological ages. Naturally, this
threw Archbishop Ussher's (1582–1629) calculations for the
age of the Earth, based on strict adherence to Genesis, out of
line, by thousands, if not millions, of years.

At about the same time, the botanist, Carl Linnaeus
(1707–78), was developing his principles for classifying
different life-forms into genera and species. His book, *The
Economy of Nature*, which marks the beginning of modern
taxonomy, was to become a basic text for naturalists
attempting systematically to classify life-forms in Europe. It
was particularly important outside Europe where missionaries, traders and naturalists were discovering a wide variety of
new plants and animals. The work of the French botanist,
George Buffon (1707–85), was also extremely important in
disseminating this new approach to, and knowledge of, the
natural world. In 1739 Buffon was appointed a keeper of the
Royal Botanical Gardens and spent the greater part of his life
cataloguing the items there and writing 36 volumes of his
Histoire Naturelle. His writing drew fire from a number of
quarters, including theologians who were becoming increasingly defensive in the face of the rising scientific evidence
directed, as they felt, against the Genesis account of creation.

One of the pioneer biologists to add his voice to a new
understanding of how life on earth emerged was Lamarck
(1744–1829). Because his theories of evolution are in conflict

with Darwin's position, little attention is paid to his work today. Yet, chronologically, his views were very significant in developing a new understanding of how life evolved on Earth. He was one of the first scientists to relate fossil remains to the living organisms that they most closely correspond to in today's world. He heightened people's awareness of the continuity between the fossil remains of primitive life-forms found in the deepest strata of rocks and more complex fossils found in later strata.

Geologists in the nineteenth century built on the work of their predecessors as more fossil remains were accumulated. Between 1830 and 1833 Charles Lyell wrote three volumes, called *Principles of Geology*, on the shape of the earth, in which he developed Hutton's principles of uniformitarianism. He insisted that all the earth's phenomena – mountains, rivers, valleys – were shaped by natural forces operating over many millenia. There was no need to posit a theory of successive catastrophes and re-creations to account for these natural phenomena as some theologians were doing in response to the new fossil evidence emerging. Lyell's work is particularly important for two reasons. First of all it gathered together many of the findings of the previous hundred years and gave form to a consensus regarding the emergence of the Earth that was developing among scientists. Secondly, it was the book that Charles Darwin took with him on the *Beagle*. Darwin made extensive use of it in his travels and for this reason it has a special place in our understanding of evolution.

Charles Darwin (1809–82) revolutionized biology and many other areas of knowledge with the publication of *The Origin of Species* in 1859. When Darwin set out on the *Beagle* he believed, like most other scientists of his time, that species were immutable. His observation of plants and animals during his travels in Latin America, the Pacific and Australia raised serious questions regarding the traditional doctrine. Many of the questions he wrestled with during and after his travels could only be answered satisfactorily if species were not immutable, but had descended from a common ancestor. In the Galapagos chain, for example, islands 600 miles off Ecuador and separated from each other by a deep ocean, Darwin found similar but distinct flora and fauna on adjacent islands. It became clear to Darwin that these closely related life-forms had developed from a common ancestor rather than through separate creations by God. Given that one accepted such evolution, the problem remained how to explain the process by which it took place over the millenia. His travels had made it abundantly clear to Darwin that evolution does not take place in a vacuum, but through a process of natural selection, where the organisms best adapted to a particular ecological niche survive and reproduce. Darwin's explanation of the process of evolution was still incomplete without Mendel's work on variation and inheritance which marks the beginning of modern genetics. Still it provided a powerful argument for the theory that all life emerged from a single source.

Many people in the religious community reacted to Darwin's theory with shock and outrage. They thought they saw in the theory of evolution a blow to the old story of the Earth as enshrined in the book of Genesis. People like Bishop Wilberforce of Oxford ridiculed the theory as an attempt by the unbelieving scientific community to dethrone humans from their place at the pinnacle of the natural world and associate them instead with lowly animals.

It would be false to insist that the religious and theological community was totally united in its opposition to the evolutionary insight that was setting other scholars on fire in disciplines as diverse as biology and sociology. Henry Drummond, a Scottish evangelical scholar and preacher, published a book entitled *Natural Law in the Spiritual World* in the 1880s. This book was immensely popular in England, the United States and much of Europe. Its wide circulation stemmed from the fact that it attempted in an attractive way to bring the insights of evolutionary science to bear on the realm of the spiritual.

A few Catholics – generally grouped together as Modernists – also tried to face up to the challenge posed by the emphasis on the natural science and historical research methods in the nineteenth century. Because they appeared to deny the possibility of objective truth and thus undermined religious truths, the movement was condemned by Pope Pius X. This condemnation in *Pascendi* (1907), and the vigorous ecclesiastical campaign which was subsequently waged to root out all vestiges of Modernism in the Catholic Church, meant that many of the questions which the Modernists posed were effectively shelved until the Second Vatican Council in the 1960s.

So while individual Christians and groups like Catholic Modernists and Protestant liberals engaged the world in which natural and social sciences were having a profound impact, still the majority of Christian thinkers failed to take up the challenge to the traditional understanding of religion. They attempted to build a wall around religion and seal it off from further attack from the empirical sciences.

Following Kant's lead, philosophers and theologians asserted that the thought processes and findings involved in studying moral and religious values were quite separate from those involved in empirical science. So the two lines of enquiry could continue on parallel tracks, while the practitioners of both extended mutual courtesies, but never really attempted to understand the challenge of each other's work. In the case of evolution, the religious world in general clung tenaciously to the Genesis account of creation understood within the framework of the discarded scientific paradigm. By taking this stand, religious understanding was impoverished by its inability to enter into creative dialogue with the emerging scientific view of the world.

The scientific community was also hampered and impoverished by the dichotomy between the secular and the sacred. Its approach to the natural world was very mechanistic. Nature was no longer alive or permeated with spirit presence. Any remaining spirit presence was quickly exorcized as the last vestige of a less enlightened age. In this process nature was objectified and shorn of any rights or inherent dignity. It was seen as crass matter, to be experimented with and manipulated to satisfy human needs and often simply human greed. As the scientific community gradually flexed its muscles in the eighteenth and nineteenth centuries, it developed a robust faith in the power of science and technology to transform the world. Science began to take on a saviour role which many believed, in time, would eliminate the need for religion. Those heady days of belief in the omnipotence of mechanistic science are gone. As the twentieth century draws to a close, the world realizes that some of the promised dreams have turned into nightmares. Nuclear weapons threaten to destroy all life on Earth. Industrial pollution is destroying air, water and soil, and the vast majority of human beings are living in poverty and subject to growing oppression and inequality.

These are the results of a mechanical view of the universe that separates the dimensions of nature and the spirit. It is worth noting, however, that modern scientific thought in biology, genetics, relativity and quantum physics challenges and repudiates much of the materialistic vision of mechanistic science. By doing so it opens up the gateway for a new era of mutually enriching interplay between science and religion which will redound to the benefit of the Earth community. But first let us look at three scientists who laid the foundations for the machine age which has profoundly shaped, and continues to affect, our modern world.

The writings of three men, Francis Bacon, René Descartes and Isaac Newton, had a profound impact in their day and the reverberation of what they wrote is still felt today. Their writings mark a 'paradigm shift' in western man's relationship with the natural world. Until this time the vast majority of people, including philosophers, looked on nature as a vital, living reality. In many societies it was seen as the locus of a numinous presence which needed to be respected and often propitiated to ensure cosmic and social harmony and peace.

The modern scientific method, which has deep roots in the writings of these three men, approached nature in a very different way. Nature was no longer permeated with spirits. It was desacralized and objectified. Having disembodied nature of its vital forces, the scientist set about understanding the laws governing nature. He did this through controlled experimentation which allowed him to formulate the laws of nature in abstract mathematical forms. Once the scientist had removed any vital inner life force from within nature and eliminated any lingering concern for moral rights that other members of the Earth community might have, the stage was set for the technologists, the captains of industry and the generals to manipulate the natural world in whatever way they pleased, to satisfy human needs, real or imaginary. The only limits to the scale and impact of the transformations were set by the power of the technology itself. Nature had no inherent rights or value; it was simply a machine put together in an extraordinary way by a Creator but with no dynamic vital principle animating it from within, such as might engage the human heart and spirit in a more profound way.

Francis Bacon (1561–1626) was one of the first on the scene, with his classic work *Novum Organum*. This work marked a decisive break with much of the intellectual tradition of the Greeks, the Romans and the Scholastics. Bacon brushed aside much of the metaphysical speculation which had preoccupied western thought for almost two thousand years. He felt it was futile to speculate on the inner constitution or nature of things. He considered that human energies would be much more productively used enquiring into how things actually work, and how they might be made to serve human beings. Knowledge was not about insight and understanding but rather about power. Power should be used to transform the Earth's resources. One could say that here, in a perverted way, was the fulfilment of the biblical injunction to exercise dominion over the Earth. The Earth was no longer endowed with mystery. It was not something to evoke awe in the enquirer or something to be communed with in love. Rather, its secrets were to be stormed, to be prised open with increasing violence, no matter what the cost to animal or plant worlds or to a large section of the human community.

Keith Thomas, in a survey of humankind's relationship with the natural world in recent centuries, makes an important point when he insists that Bacon's vision did not arise from a secularist vision of the world. Rather for Bacon 'the purpose of science was to restore to man the dominion over the creation which he had partly lost at the Fall' (page 27).[3] It is important to stress here that a religious basis for one's vision of the Earth does not necessarily mean that one's relationship with the Earth will be benign and mutually enhancing. As we will see on many occasions in this book, it may well have the opposite effect.

Bacon, in a posthumously published book called *New Atlantis* (1627), advocated setting up an academy to put this vision into practice. The school would have a much more practical orientation than the universities where, Bacon argued, only theoretical issues were studied. This academy would include lecture facilities, a good library, research facilities, workshops and a power house to transform the knowledge into usable technology. The emphasis was on using the knowledge to transform the Earth. Bacon himself wrote: 'The end of our Foundation is the knowledge of causes, and the secret motions of things, and the enlarging of the bounds of the human empire, *to the effecting of all things possible.*'[4] (Italics mine.)

Bacon set two important waves in motion in the western world which have continued to gather power and momentum ever since. First, his ideas released enormous psychic energies, mainly within the scientific community, to study, record and correlate the secrets of the Earth, no matter what the cost to living beings, including the scientist. They also legitimized the pursuit of knowledge for its own sake, irrespective of any reflection on the meaning of the knowledge or how that knowledge might be used. In our own day this dichotomy between the pursuit of knowledge and the use that might be made of it is very clear in such fields as nuclear physics, chemical engineering and genetics. The standard scientific training for scientists engaged in this research does not generally include any serious reflection on the nature of the power which they are unlocking, or ethical considerations regarding the context in which this power may be used.

The narrow definition of the scientist's task was illustrated in the Manhattan project during World War II. The scientist's role was to scale the ramparts of knowledge, acquire the secrets of nature, by whatever means were necessary, and finally communicate that knowledge. The use to which the new knowledge might be put does not fall within the domain of the scientist. It is for the philosopher, the theologian, the politician or someone else, with little understanding of the awesome power involved, to decide. Today many people, including scientists themselves, see that this dichotomy is actually a recipe for disasters of enormous magnitude.

Descartes (1596–1650) was both a mathematician and a philosopher. His central contribution was to insist on the importance of mathematics for understanding and stating in a concise and orderly way the laws governing nature. He argued that the mathematical method should be developed and expanded to include all reality. The empirical scientist should move in this direction in order to bring measurement, precision, order and predictability to the study of all reality. This discipline was essential in order that controlled experimentation might discover universal, objective laws. Building on this insight of Descartes, it was understandable that, in the centuries that followed, the sciences that seemed most susceptible to accurate computation, like physics, enjoyed a pre-eminent status. The scientific method employed in these sciences became the norm for every other science.

This insight has yielded many benefits to a certain segment of humanity, yet the cost to the Earth community over the past few centuries has been enormous. While mathematics and cold rationality endow the human being with great power to understand and manipulate quantitative relationships, they cannot deal with qualitative judgements. Therefore they either dismiss them as unimportant or attempt to reduce them to measurable quantities. Colour, taste, warmth, smell, joy, pain are often forgotten. In the mechanistic scientific community a cold, somewhat disapproving eye is often cast on sciences such as biology, psychology, sociology and anthropology where quantification is hard to come by and, even if precise measurements can be taken, very often they do not mean much. Even so, this fascination with numbers has affected practitioners of these sciences. More and more in psychology and anthropology one finds an obsession with statistics and mathematical relationships which very often cloud rather than facilitate any insight into life or human ways of knowing or relating.

This craving to reduce everything to mathematical formulae can be traced back to Descartes. All of nature—insects, plants, animals and even the human body—is seen simply as a machine governed by universal mechanical laws which can be stated with mathematical precision. Descartes argued that his emphasis on logic, mathematics and measurement would unlock the secrets of nature for the benefit of human beings. 'As distinctly as we understand the various trades of our artisans, and by application of this knowledge to any use to which it is adapted, we could make ourselves masters and *possessors of nature*'.[5] (Italics mine.)

The power which Descartes bequeathed to the human community to bring mathematical rigour to scientific experimentation was quickly seized upon by the architects of the emerging technical age to effect a wholesale transformation of nature when the technology to do so became available. In the world that was about to be shaped by this insight and drive, everything from the smallest particle to human work was to be measured in units of time, space and energy.

Sir Isaac Newton (1642–1727) was the third person to contribute to the contours of the emerging mechanical paradigm. Newton is such a significant figure in the development of modern scientific knowledge that he is often considered the father of modern science. In his famous work *Principia* he published his discoveries on terrestrial and celestial mechanics. His most significant advance on other observers of the celestial spheres was to bring mathematical precision to the laws of motion. The predictability of the principle of universal gravitation explains both the motion of falling bodies on Earth and the movement of planets in the heavens.

Newton's universe closely resembles a complex, finely calibrated machine, with the parts interlocking according to the laws of cause and effect. In fact, it closely resembled a clock which, as the first automatic machine, played an important role in developing a clockwork model of the universe.

When one moved from the skies back to Earth the clock model was still effective. The world was highly stratified, with inanimate matter at the bottom and then, on tier after tier, the plants, insects, animals, until the impartial observer reached an unbridgeable gap. Beyond this gap, at the top of the pyramid and absolutely superior to it, sat the human. Intelligence gave a superior position to human beings, and in the process downgraded the natural world. There is no talk in this vision of the universe of a life-community with close relationship between living species; there is no idea of a closely-related family where damage to one species is seen as damage to the whole. Rather the universe and the Earth were there to be used solely for and by human beings.

This 'mechanical' view of the universe proved enormously attractive to western man during the eighteenth, nineteenth and twentieth centuries. It provided a framework of perception and a stimulus for inventors to develop new, more powerful and, in this view, more efficient technologies to transform and process the Earth. With the Industrial Revolution the power and scale of these technologies increased enormously. Today, the chemical, nuclear and engineering industries seem to have a power of their own and are scarring the Earth, poisoning water, air and soil, killing off life-forms and threatening to let loose a fireball which will engulf the planet and destroy every living being.

The mechanical paradigm does not merely goad *Homo Faber* to create new machines in order, more effectively and efficiently, to process the planet. It has affected the way we view everything on Earth. The writings of men like John Locke and Adam Smith have influenced our understanding of political and economic realities. The present indicators we use for judging whether an economy is booming – Gross National Product (GNP) – merely tell us the speed at which the manufacturing and service sectors take the natural resources, process them, speed them as quickly as possible through a consumer economy and within a few short years discard them on a junk heap. GNP indicators do not tell us about the interchange of goods and services between all species of the life-community, and whether the life-community is itself booming or is being preyed upon by a single species to the point where the whole system may collapse. It does not even record what percentage of a particular human community is benefiting by this destruction.

As the rate of exploitation increases by means of improved technology and more efficient organizations, management indicators record an improved rating for individual enterprises and the whole industrial economy. In this view, management does not see itself as having any responsibility for the total Earth community, even though in any adequate accounting system this is really the bottom line. If we continue to plunder the Earth, every commercial operation will eventually collapse. Destruction, not profits, will be the common lot for everyone.

David Noble's *America by Design*[6] is an excellent account of how the machine metaphor has transformed the United States and, because of the importance of the American economy, almost the entire globe in the past one hundred years. The transformation has touched all facets of life beginning with the extractive industries, and moving on to manufacturing industry, agriculture, working conditions, advertising, human relations and even human self-perception. Noble describes how, after 1860, scientific technology and corporate capitalism transformed and reshaped every facet of life. He maintains that the impetus came in the main from mechanical engineers. Until 1860 mechanical engineers received most of their training through being apprenticed to skilled mechanics. There was little need for a sophisticated theoretical training because the major tasks of making even a steam engine were not very complex.

All this changed with the rise of the petrochemical and electrical industries in the United States around the 1880s. The engineers in these industries needed a thorough theoretical and technical training so that the power of the scientific imagination could be brought to bear more directly on the practical problems of these infant industries. In order to keep pace with competitors, the chemical, electrical and automotive industries needed research and design departments. The engineers who staffed these industries received specialized training in the applied as well as in the pure sciences.

The captains of industry were not enthusiastic about the way the traditional universities and colleges responded to their demands. Harvard and Yale and other established universities still gave pride of place to the humanities and to scientific theory. The corporations felt that much of this knowledge was irrelevant and so they set up their own technical schools. The first and most famous of these, the Massachusetts Institute of Technology (MIT) was founded in 1861, and set a pattern for a host of similar institutes, first in the United States and then all round the world. A branch of the Mindanao State University in Iligan City is called The Iligan Institute of Technology.

Graduates from these schools have transformed the natural world, building dams, bridges, steel mills, chemical plants, nuclear power stations and a deadly arms manufacturing industry. But, according to Noble's thesis, the engineers were not content to transform inanimate objects. They set about 'engineering' people to be both efficient cogs in the industrial process and passive recipients of the goods of the consumer economy. This is evident in the demands for rationalization and standardization at the pit-heads of the mines. It is found in the mass production procedures which were developed for the automotive industry and are now found in most assembly lines.

In an earlier phase of the Industrial Revolution, Karl Marx (1818-1883) saw how alienating these processes could be for the workers, since they have no part in the decisions which affect their lives and little access to the capital their labour creates. Though the working conditions and living standards of workers have improved considerably in First-World countries, the alienation which results from putting machines before workers is still very much a problem in many countries. Pope John Paul II called attention to it in the encyclical *Laborem Exercens*[7] when he said that the worker must be the 'subject' and not the 'object' of the productive process.

The manufacturing cycle is completed by the techniques of Madison Avenue. Massive advertising campaigns manipulate consumers and create demands. The soft drinks industry set the trend; Coca-Cola budgets a huge percentage of its turnover for advertising. The campaign induces millions of people to drink a beverage which has little nutritional value and a high sugar content which can even be bad for a person's health. The advertising campaign can also make people greedy. People are valued, not for what they are in themselves, but for what they own.

Noble argues that in industrialized countries a profound change has taken place in the way human beings live, work and even think about themselves. This is not an unintended by-product, but was planned, with strategies worked out to achieve it. Noble quotes a top executive of the National Cash Register Company in 1913 who made no secret of his ultimate desire – 'I am most interested in increasing the efficiency of the human machine.'

The change in metaphorical language from living beings to machines reinforces the tendency to hold up the machine as the image for ourselves and all living reality. It is the final step in the trend set almost four centuries ago. It is now so deep in our consciousness that we hardly notice it anymore, as Wendell Berry points out in *The Gift of Good Land*.

> Until the industrial revolution occurred, in the minds of most people in the so-called 'developed' countries the dominant images were organic; they had to do with living things, they were biological, pastoral, agricultural or familial. God was seen as a 'shepherd', the faithful as 'the sheep of his pasture'. People who took care of the earth were said to practice 'husbandry'. Now we do not flinch to hear men and women referred to as 'units' as if they were machines. It is common, and considered acceptable, to refer to the mind as a 'computer', one's thoughts as 'inputs', other people's responses as feedback.[8]

These changes in human living which have been brought about in the main by corporate technology have also left their scars on the Earth, as we have seen many times already. No one, of course, would accuse corporate technology of consciously setting out to plunder and poison the planet. In fact the chemical industry, for example, sees itself as a benefactor providing food for the hungry. The nuclear industry sees itself in the forefront of those supplying industrial and domestic power. Even the arms industry proclaims itself as the peacekeeper of the human community. Each of the major industries in the modern world probably sees itself, and is often perceived by others, as ushering in a new age of plenty, joy, happiness, pleasure and peace. But behind the glittering image, the Earth keeps a different record. During the past century and, especially since World War II, we have been creating a lonely, squalid and silent world.

5

THE NEW STORY

How, we may ask, can the human community free itself from the grip of the machine metaphor? Its many benefits have seduced and dazzled us. Unfortunately, those of us who have benefitted most from the labour-saving inventions of modern technology are often not conscious of the negative aspects of technology. We fail to record accurately what the ever-increasing web of technology has done to the vast majority of people in Third-World countries and to the Earth itself. We need a much deeper understanding of technology before we let loose its power in our world. In other words, we need a new context of meaning for technology which will allow us to pinpoint those technologies which enhance life on Earth and those which retard it. In order to do this effectively, we need a new understanding of the story of life on Earth and the creative role which human beings and their artifacts must play in that story.

In a word, there is a need for a new story or myth of the emergence of the Earth. Since the dawn of human consciousness, story has been the basic vehicle of human understanding and meaning. In every culture, throughout history, storytellers have enthralled and delighted people and brought joy and meaning to their lives.

The 'story' which I will present here is a story of our universe which comes to us through modern ways of knowing. Strange as it might seem, since storytelling is not often associated with the discourse of science, the tellers of this story are the scientists. They have shaped and refined an intelligible and exciting new story of our universe. The sequence of the story is not the work of any single scientist but is the cooperative venture of many individual scientists and scientific disciplines. The astronomers who have gazed with wonder on the night sky with their ever more powerful telescopes have joined with physicists who have studied the minute particles of matter. To clarify important elements of the story, biologists and geneticists have spent long hours examining living tissue. Sometimes the whole scientific community has moved forward, piecing together the most fascinating and stupendous story ever told.

The task of fashioning the story continues. Even with satellite probings of the heavens and explorations into the depths of the oceans, the picture is by no means complete. Nevertheless, the broad outlines are there, and the story is revealing itself as one of extraordinary creativity, variation, abundance and beauty.

More important, this is our story, one which gives the Earth community, and especially human beings, a breadth and depth hitherto undreamed of. It is truly a revolutionary story and confirms, without a shadow of doubt, that the universe does not run on mechanistic principles. All the processes of nature, from the emergence of life itself to the cycle of the seasons and the metabolic processes of living forms, are intimately related. This new story is a powerful antidote to the mechanistic story of the past four hundred years. It shows the old story to be shallow in comparison to the new one's magnificent span of twenty billion years. It also tells us that unless we abandon mechanistic science and technology we place in jeopardy the future florescence of this beautiful Earth. It tells us that to attempt to understand human beings outside the context of the emergent universe is to restrict ourselves unduly and to hamper any genuine effort at self-understanding, either as individuals or as a species. This new story must, more and more, begin to shape our lives, even our religious sensibilities, and it must provide norms of behaviour for human activity. Above all it provides the spiritual energies for the whole human community to begin to live according to the dictates of the story.

We have seen that the physical and biological articulation of the story gradually emerged from the scientific community during the later part of the nineteenth century and the early twentieth century. Partly because of the antipathy and misunderstanding between the scientific community and most religious people, one essential dimension was missing. The story lacked spiritual understanding.

It took the genius and courage of Pierre Teilhard de Chardin (1881–1955) – a priest and paleontologist – to bridge this gap. Teilhard insisted that any complete telling of the story of the universe must include its psychic dimension, otherwise the presentation will be fragmented and would fail to situate human beings in a proper cosmic context. Teilhard felt that much of the alienation experienced by the intellectual community in the twentieth century stemmed from a too-restricted understanding of the human trajectory. For Teilhard, however, the universe, the Earth and human ventures were far from absurd. From the first moment of the universe twenty billion years ago, every particle of matter carried within itself the seeds of everything that was to emerge in later unfoldings, including human consciousness. Any telling of the universe story which fails to speak adequately about the 'within' of things is radically defective and will end in a dualism that human beings will find alienating.

So Teilhard set about telling the story of the 'without' and 'within' of things in a single synthesis. Using the idiom of contemporary scientists, Teilhard, according to Mircea Eliade, the doyen of comparative religion scholars, was 'the first Christian author to present his faith in terms accessible and meaningful to the agnostic scientist and to the religiously illiterate in general'.[1] His overall synthesis, which is worked out in *The Phenomenon of Man*, is far reaching and powerful. In the words of Julian Huxley in his introduction to the book, Teilhard has 'effected a threefold synthesis – of the material and physical world with the world of mind and spirit; of the past with the future; and of variety with unity, the many with the one.'[2]

According to Teilhard the galaxies, the solar system and the Earth unfolded through a dramatic variety of sequences – from the initial energy in the 'primaeval atom', through the synthesization of matter in the first generation of stars, to the birth of life on planet Earth, and finally to human consciousness itself. With the increased complexification of matter through successive transformations, there is a corresponding increase in interiorization.[3] Each unfolding, however, is elaborated within the fullness of the complete presentation of the story. In fact it only finds its full meaning when seen as part of the whole story. The full potential of heavier atoms, for example, is revealed through their role in developing and sustaining life and ultimately in human consciousness. This is why Teilhard traces the roots of the human right back to the very beginning and insists that now the full dynamism of the evolutionary process is contained within the human.[4] The human being is the key to understanding the entire evolutionary process. One cannot, for example, reduce everything that preceded the human to crass matter, as mechanistic science often does, and maintain that consciousness is only a dimension of the final stage of the process. This would mean that the glory of all the yearnings and strivings of the evolutionary process was merely an afterthought.

The human being, however, is no intruder within the Earth community, but in the words of Julian Huxley, which Teilhard quotes, 'man discovers that he is nothing else than evolution become conscious of itself'.[5] Every aspect of the human, including the human mind, is as much Earth as the mountains, rivers, animals, birds and other members of the Earth community. By concentrating on the psychic dimension from the very beginning and keeping it continually in focus, Teilhard overcomes the dualistic, materialistic approach which has underpinned much of the classical Newtonian scientific tradition. The breadth and depth of his thought establishes the emergent universe as a vital, living and closely related reality. In the human being, this universe reveals itself most intensely and fully.

Modern scientists like Lewis Thomas and James Lovelock add their voices to this perspective. According to Thomas, the Earth, looked at from a distance over a long period of time, appears like an embryogenesis. This unified view of the Earth as a living planet – the garden planet of the universe – is seen in the photographs which satellites have relayed back to Earth. They show a beautiful blue Earth, the habitat for all creatures, and are now commonplace in many books and posters. These photos have an impact on anyone who takes time to reflect on their implications. They put into perspective all the petty conflicts that divide the human community and remind us that human beings are part of the family of the living.

Lovelock, a British scientist who worked for The National

Aeronautics and Space Administration (NASA), put forward his famous *Gaia* hypothesis soon after the first landing on the moon.[6] This theory postulates that the entire chain of living beings, from simple bacteria to human beings, are interconnected and can be viewed as a single entity. This living entity possesses powers beyond those of its constitutive parts. Like the human body which can control temperature through homeostatic mechanisms, this entity, which he calls *Gaia* – recalling the Earth personified as a goddess in Greek mythology – has mechanisms which optimize the conditions suitable for life. Evidence in this direction is the fact that the oxygen content of the air was stabilized at about twenty-one percent and the temperature of the Earth has remained stable for hundreds of millions of years.

So from a variety of sources this vision of an evolving Earth must today become the norm of what is real and worth striving for within every institution on the planet. Human beings must enter as creatively as possible into the processes of the planet in order to discern the true role of the human within the Earth's story. This emergent story will give the human community basic norms to guide the human–Earth relationship in a way that will be mutually enriching and enhancing. These norms must be enshrined in our political, economic, social, commercial and religious institutions so that these enhance the Earth community and do not impoverish it.

Before going on to look at some of the sequences of the new story it is worth calling attention to the fact that Teilhard's insight will involve a major shift in emphasis for western Christianity's theological and spiritual tradition. Since the late Middle Ages and particularly since the Reformation, there has been an almost exclusive concentration in western theological tradition on a Fall/Redemption theology, much of which can be traced back to Augustine.

This theological tradition has no adequate theology of creation. The twenty billion years of God's creative love is simply seen either as the stage on which the drama of human salvation is worked out, or as something radically sinful in itself and needing transformation. Teilhard's most important contribution to religion is to shift the balance in order to include a contemporary understanding of creation. He interprets the Cosmic Christ theme of St Paul and St John in the light of the story of the emergent cosmos. He is convinced that religion in the twentieth century needs to be grounded on our new understanding of cosmic evolution if it is to be meaningful to men and women of our time. In this way Teilhard gives to the story as told by scientists a sacred and religious significance. He is convinced that this is imperative if it is to transform human consciousness. I will return to discussion of the religious significance of the story in Chapter 6.

Despite some difficulties with various aspects of Teilhard's thought which tend to disturb more orthodox scientists and theologians, and his own somewhat uncritical belief in the goodness and inevitability of technological progress, he has indicated for us a new story of the universe which should guide all our endeavours today.

The sequence of the story which I present here is filling out and adapting the Teilhardian schema which Thomas Berry uses in *The New Story*.[7] This includes the Galactic, Earth, Life and Human Consciousness phases of the story of the universe.

The Story of the Universe

The story of the universe begins for each human being as soon as we look with wonder, awe and curiosity at the world around us. As we begin to learn about the story from the scientists, the universe reveals itself to us in surprising ways. If we fix our eyes on the nearest mountain, or better still, gaze into the heavens on a starry night, we might be inclined to think that the world, at least the physical world, is permanent. Nothing could be further from the truth. Teilhard in the *Phenomenon of Man*, echoing modern scientific probings into the origins of the universe, tells us that the primary feature of the story is one of change and transformation. True, the time-scale for the transformations is enormous and the space immense. The figures involved are often beyond what our human sense of time and space can comprehend, but still they tell us that we live in an evolving universe. The challenge of our times is to understand how this insight can chart our course in today's world. What follows are some broad outlines of that story.

Today the consensus in the scientific community is that the universe did have a beginning. It began somewhere between fifteen and twenty billion years ago in a radiation-dominated 'primaeval atom' of enormous density. Yet enfolded in this 'primaeval atom' were all the potentialities of what was to follow through myriads of transformations throughout the history of the universe. This primaeval atom exploded in what has become known as the Big Bang. (I do not particularly like the term as it robs this most sacred event of all mystery and poetry.)

The initial explosion sent 'matter' exploding outwards in all directions. The explosion itself is remarkable. Scientists like Sir Bernard Lovell tell us that if the universe had emerged a fraction of a second faster or slower it would have exploded in such a way that it could never coalesce into galaxies at a later stage, or it would have collapsed back on itself. So in its initial moment, a sacred moment in the epics of most peoples, the universe came into existence at a slim – almost zero – margin of possibility. This fact, and the many other extremely important transformations, like that from non-life to life, which again took place at almost zero possibility, tell us something about the fragility of the universe. And yet there is obviously an enduring reality. Scientists have discovered in recent years that the glow of that initial explosion still shines over all reality in the solar system.

During and after the initial explosion, matter as we know it did not exist. As the universe expanded and simultaneously cooled, protons and neutrons fused into atomic nuclei of hydrogen and helium. Gradually, as the expansion and cooling continued, electrons joined with the nuclei to form atoms and matter as we know it was born. The atoms and molecules, which constitute the Sun, the planets and all living organisms on Earth, were parts of some star billions of years ago. The galaxies were formed out of the original hydrogen cloud. These enormous clouds scattered in space coalesced together; under gravitational pressures they tended to collapse in on themselves. As the temperature rose, they ignited nuclear fires at their core, and thus the stars were born. The nuclear processes transform hydrogen into helium. At present, for example, the sun transforms hydrogen into helium at the rate of 4.5 million tons per second. Stars like our sun continue the transformation process until the supply of hydrogen is exhausted, then they often shrink and die. If the galaxies were composed only of small or medium sized stars, the heavier elements like carbon, phosphorus, sulphur and iron which are essential for life, would never have emerged at the core. It took the supernovas to synthesize these elements at their core and a dying gasp, as it were, to spew the elements out into space where they could once again coalesce.

Some five to ten billion years ago, our solar system was born as a diffuse cloud of dust and gas from the debris of an earlier generation of stars. The original solar nebula broke up into distinct areas of turbulence. Large segments of matter clustered together at varying distances from the proto-sun. As these clusters continued to rotate, their gravitational field attracted smaller planets and meteorites and so they coalesced into larger planets. The process continued until the planets as we know them began to take shape. The basic structure was a solid core of matter surrounded by a dense atmosphere of hydrogen and helium. Once the gravitational pressures set off the thermonuclear reaction in the sun, the intense radiation swept away much of the hydrogen and helium in the original atmosphere of the Earth.

The Earth

The Earth is, as I have said, the garden planet of the universe. As far as we know it is the only planet that can support life and it does so in extraordinary profusion, abundance and variety. It does not support life from its own resources alone. The Earth took shape at just the right distance from the sun, close enough for the sun's heat and energy to make conditions hospitable for life, and yet not so close as to smother everything, as happened in the case of Mercury and Venus.

Scientists estimate that the Earth came into being about 4.6 billion years ago. Originally it was cold; however, the interior began to heat up under gravitational pressures. These pressures were not great enough to light a nuclear core, as happened in the stars. Rather the increased temperature and pressures led to the formation of a molten nickel and iron core. In this way the planet began to take on a stratified shape during its early evolution. Heavy metals sank to the centre and lighter metals rose to the top. This top layer, the Earth's crust, is a relatively thin skin of rock with lighter metals riding on the mantle below. Many geologists today believe that the crust is made up of a number of plates which drift apart and collide, thrusting up mountains like the Andes in Latin America and the Himalayas. Beneath the crust is the mantle, comprising most of the volume of the Earth and extending from 20 or 30 kilometres to 2000 kilometres. Below the mantle is the core.

The Earth is not sedate today, and certainly was not so in its infancy. Numerous rings of volcanoes all around the world continually released gases and magma to create over millions of years the atmosphere and the oceans. The stabilization of the oceans was a significant milestone in the history of the planet Earth, as the oceans are both the birthplace and the early cradle for life on the planet.

The emergence of a free-oxygen atmosphere is also vital for any higher life-forms. The original atmosphere was dominated by carbon monoxide. This was burned off by the increase both in the heat from the core and the sun's heat. The formation of a new atmosphere began as the Earth cooled. Volcanoes continued to emit gases and vapour in the form of hydrogen, carbon, nitrogen and oxygen. In the cooling process, hydrogen combined with oxygen to form water.

All the chemical elements that compose living matter were present in the 'soup' of the primordial oceans. How the inert mixture underwent the numerous chemical reactions to produce the first organic molecule is not yet clear. The process probably involved considerable electric energy from cosmic radiation. Once the living molecule was able to reproduce itself, life on Earth was possible. The small marine micro-organisms which emerged in the ocean played an important role in releasing oxygen into the air, yet to reproduce and propagate they began to feed on the original ocean 'soup', so that it seemed life would be snuffed out in its very infancy. But once again the creativities deep within the Earth responded and the important process of photosynthesis, the use of solar energy to transform non-living matter into living tissue, and regulate the oxygen content of the air, began. These early plants and their descendants have ensured that the percentage of oxygen in the air is maintained by photosynthesis at around twenty-one percent. Without photosynthesis, animals like ourselves would lack the capacity to transform non-living beings into chemical energy could not survive. Photosynthesis was a step in the process which would in time lead to lung-breathing creatures who would emerge from the oceans to walk on the Earth or fly through the air.

Photosynthesis is also essential for the maintenance of the biosphere, as it allows organic life to transform inanimate matter and use it to reproduce cells. The chemical structure of all cells, whether in the leaves of trees, the fishes in the sea, the grass in the field or the human brain, is quite similar. This indicates that plants and animals, despite enormous diversity, spring from the same origin and are intimately related. All living beings are members of a single extended family.

This brief outline of some of the central moments in the evolution of the Earth should give us much food for thought. The first consideration is the time-scale involved in creating the atmosphere and the oceans so that they could give birth to and support life. The second is that our industrial processes have in a few short decades changed the chemical composition of the air and flushed billions of tonnes of poisonous filth and garbage into the oceans. Flushing our waste into the sea is increasingly causing worry to scientists, as we saw in Chapter 2. Thor Heyerdahl's comment – that since life on land is so utterly dependent on life in the sea, we can safely deduce that a dead sea means a dead planet – should cause us to stop and reflect seriously on what we are doing to the life-support system of the planet.

In the formation of the stars, the sun, the Earth and the birth of life we have a marvellous sequence of transformations. Beginning with the compressed, extremely hot, dense energy of the original fireball these unfoldings go through an almost infinite number of sequences, from the shaping of the first atom, to the emergence of life on the planet, culminating in human life. In the human, a being endowed with self-consciousness, the whole universe reflects upon itself and celebrates its own wonderful journey. Not only did the elements that compose human bodies take shape in the dying embers of supernova explosions but so also did human minds, since the 'within' of things is co-extensive with the total development of the universe.

It is important to remember the extraordinary length of time – billions of years – involved in the emergence of the universe and the birth and florescence of life-forms that we see around us today. While human beings may consider themselves as the high point of the evolutionary process, we need to remember that we are creatures of relatively recent origin. The oldest fossil remains of hominoid types are only about five million years old, and our own species, *Homo sapiens sapiens*, is much more recent. Our relative youth should make us careful about interfering with the life dynamics of the planet. We should be careful not to introduce toxic substances like DDT into the Earth's system. The Earth's own natural production of chemicals avoided such compounds, presumably for very good reasons. As we saw in Chapters 2 and 3, many man-made substances are now endangering life in almost every corner of the globe.

To grasp the impact of human activity, particularly since the beginning of the Industrial Revolution, it might help to put the Earth's story in a time-scale which we can comprehend. If the total history of the universe were somehow compressed into a single year, human beings would appear on Earth at 11 pm on the 365th day. The Industrial Revolution, which is having such a deleterious impact on the biosphere would take place during the last half-second of the year.

We also notice that life did not evolve on an unchanging Earth. The emergence of life prepared the way for more and more complex life-forms. As we have seen above, the emergence of the hydrosphere and the free-oxygen atmosphere was a *sine qua non* for the emergence of higher life-forms. Regard for this delicate interplay of life-forms supporting the web of life today should halt our tendency to pollute the sky or the seas. In many cases we have no idea what the long-term effects might be. By the time the changes are perceptible, as in the case of the 'greenhouse' effect, it might be too late to reverse the damage.

This brings us to another important element in the story

which we tend to forget. The sequences of transformation which form the story of the universe are irreversible. We are so used to life-forms renewing themselves through birth, and the sequence of the seasons, that we seldom reflect on the irreversibility of the evolutionary process. Yet, as Teilhard puts it in the *Phenomenon of Man:* 'once and only once in the course of its planetary existence has the Earth been able to envelope itself with life. Similarly, once and only once has life succeeded in crossing the threshold of reflection. For thought as for life there has been just one season.'[8]

We need to take a hard look at what is involved in irreversibility because modern industrial cultures is not establishing a sustainable way of life for the human community. We are using more and more of the Earth's resources and living in a way that is extinguishing thousands of species of plants and animals and endangering hundreds of thousands of others. We need to realize that the planetary system, at least on Earth, is vulnerable to human activity. The human community must now become aware of how crucial its behaviour is for the well-being of the community of life on Earth. Rather than acting as parasites, human beings must now assume their proper function as the heart and mind of the *Gaia* and thereby optimize the conditions necessary for all life on Earth.

An illustration on pages 154 and 155 of *Gaia* presents at a single view the sequence of some of the most important unfoldings of life on Earth. The artist depicts the flame of life beginning almost 3,500 million years ago in the earliest microfossils. For many hundreds of millions of years the flame smouldered very precariously as the conditions necessary for more abundant life were slowly created. The free-oxygen atmosphere and the ozone layer which protected simple life-forms from the ultra-violet rays of the sun built up around 2,000 million years ago. During a period of about 1,000 million years, life developed the ability to reproduce sexually and to feed upon itself. This gave a powerful impetus to the flame of life. Fossil remains show that the first invertebrates appeared during the Cambrian period, about 570 million years ago.

There were major periods of extinction both at the end of

the Permian period, about 226 million years ago, and at the end of the Cretaceous period, about 65 million years ago. Still the life flame always leaped back, strengthened and more diversified, with better developed strategies for reproduction and survival. As we will see below, mammalian life would not have flourished if the dinosaurs had not become extinct 65 million years ago.

A major milestone in the story was passed when life-forms moved ashore. This took place probably in estuaries and shallow seas. It demanded new skills so that the new life-forms did not dry up and die, and they also had to acquire the ability to breathe oxygen. Some of the early colonizers were amphibians, mosses and liverworts. These latter were the precursors of the gymnosperms (non-flowering plants) which dominated the Carboniferous age around 345 million years ago, and the angiosperms (flowering plants) which proliferated during the Cretaceous period, around 130 million years ago.

Reptiles, especially dinosaurs, dominated the Earth between about 200 and 65 million years ago, when they disappeared quite abruptly, for reasons which are not yet completely clear. It does appear now that a meteor may have collided with the Earth. This in turn may have set off a fireball which engulfed much of the vegetation in the northern hemisphere; the resulting nuclear-winter type of environment caused the extinction of the large reptiles. Once the dinosaurs disappeared, mammalian life blossomed. The warm-blooded mammals had developed new strategies for reproducing, within the body of the mother. As warm-blooded animals, their ability to control their body temperature increased their ability to move to different climatic regions of the Earth. New survival skills were evident in the emergence of primates. Their stereoscopic vision and well-adapted gripping mechanism were particularly suited to living in the forest.

The Emergence of Human Beings

There is much discussion among paleontologists and archeologists about how and where *Homo sapiens* emerged.

Much of the research in recent decades has been carried out in East Africa. The efforts to uncover the origins of human beings have attracted widespread interest; the latest findings are always liable to find their way into *Time* or the latest edition of *Reader's Digest*.

The picture that is emerging from recent research pushes back the emergence of humanoid creatures to four million years ago. There are three forms – *Australopithecus, Homo erectus* and *Homo sapiens. Australopithecus* lived in Africa until about one million years ago. Despite a heavy brow ridge and protruding jaw, they resemble modern human beings in their physical structure. They walked upright, had increased brain capacity and fashioned crude tools. *Homo erectus*, now extinct, are thought to have been contemporaries of *Australopithecus*. Their brain capacity was larger, their tools were more advanced and they had also developed the beginnings of social organization. For thousands of years *Homo erectus* lived in the same area as their successors *Homo sapiens*, who again had a larger brain capacity, around 1350cc. Two now extinct races of *Homo sapiens* emerge from excavations in many parts of the world – *Neanderthal* and *Cro-Magnon. Neanderthal* was widespread in Africa, Asia and the Mediterranean area of Europe. They lived in caves, were hunters and quite proficient tool-makers. *Cro-Magnon* fossils are found in Europe, dating from about 30,000 years ago. They possessed a more developed technology, a variety of art forms and religious beliefs regarding the dead. This brings us right up to the period of *Homo sapiens sapiens*.

Then came the tribal age, a period of creativity for the human community. Human beings established themselves around the world. This was the real age of discovery, not the fifteenth century of the Christian era as is often suggested. A wide variety of languages, and social, political, moral and religious systems also emerged during this spring-time of human creativity. Tribal peoples created the world of myth, and they identified and shaped many of the archetypal structures of human consciousness which still guide our secular and religious life today. Among these are the myth of the great hero, the journey symbol, both within the human psyche and across the landscape of the Earth, and the symbol of a sacred place. The contours of the world of the spirits were also laid down. These operated to guide the community in its relationship to the natural and the supernatural worlds.

Most of the basic food sources which we still use today were discovered during the tribal era. Today scientists are beginning to appreciate the immense store of wisdom which tribal peoples have evolved and accumulated over the millenia. Tribal cultures have endured over a long period. They would not have survived had they not developed a harmonious relationship with the natural world around them. Though in our ignorance we often look on the tribal phase of the human venture as a primitive moment, one could say that the foundations and parameters of what it means to be human were established at this time.

With the domestication of plants and animals, the increase in population density, the introduction of agricultural technologies like irrigation and the development of metallurgy and pottery, the Great Civilization emerged first in Mesopota-mia some 5,500 years ago, later on in Harappa on the banks of the Indus river, in China and in the Mayan and Aztec civilizations of Mesoamerica. Religion played an important part in developing these civilizations. The shrines, temples and priestly castes often played a significant role in the social, political and economic life as well. These civilizations also gave rise to the great classical religions, Hinduism, Buddhism, Judaism, Christianity and Islam, which have in turn profoundly shaped our moral and religious consciousness. Many of the moral principles which still influence our actions today were fashioned in this period.

Written languages helped solve the organizational challenge which more numerous and far-flung cultures posed to political and commercial leaders. The written word also enabled society to record its cherished myths, stories, poetry and liturgies and promulgate its laws, and also to plot the movements of heavenly bodies, which in turn led to the development of the calendar. The development and refine-ment of the calendar was a milestone in the Earth–human relations, allowing individuals and whole societies to integrate themselves more intimately into the rhythms of nature. It also gave to the human actor a measure of control and the power to predict the sequences of the natural world, which was a boon to the farming community.

Another important legacy of this era is the attention given to developing abstract thought. This is found in all civilizations: Greek thinkers pursued the idea of the Logos, the idea of the Tao emerged in China, while a quest for ultimate reality or Brahman engaged many thoughtful people in India.

Finally, the era of the great civilizations saw the beginning and gradual increase of world-wide commerce, and the infancy of scientific endeavours. In an extensive way, many of the great historic civilizations developed in isolation from each other. Since the western colonial expansion to every corner of the globe in the sixteenth century, civilizations have come more and more into contact with each other. Teilhard calls this mutually enriching contact with many traditions on a global scale 'planetization'. It means that no matter where our own cultural roots are, almost every person on Earth is affected today by the convergence of civilized traditions. It recognizes that the human community needs the wisdom and knowledge of each of these traditions to nourish and sustain us into the future.

In a brief 150 years, the industrial age, whose foundations were laid by the work of Bacon, Descartes and Newton, has gone through a number of phases. It began with coal and steam. Then Thomas Edison's discoveries regarding the use of electricity, and the discovery and use of oil in the later part of the nineteenth century, led to the electrical and petrochemical phase of the industrial age. The nuclear age began literally with a bang, with the dropping of the first atom bomb on Hiroshima on 6 August 1945. Today much of humanity lives in fear of being incinerated by a nuclear holocaust or of contacting cancer from nuclear waste. While one cannot deny that some of the comforts and benefits of this age have helped ease the toil of life for many, the benefits come at enormous cost. The industrial age has changed the chemistry, geology and biology of the planet Earth and affected every preceding phase of the story of the universe in an irreversible way.

The Age of GAIA

Gradually the human community is beginning to wake up to what is happening to the Earth and to view it in a less exploitative way. Scott Carpenter's photos of the Earth taken from space may well be a turning point in our understanding and respect for the Earth. We see it suspended in the sky, and realize that the Earth, seas, air, sky, sunlight and living forms are established in a single functional planetary system so unified and interrelated that a scientist like Lewis Thomas can say that the closest analogy to the biosphere is the single living cell.

During the past fifteen years, many individuals and groups have begun to take seriously the message of the new story. Rachel Carson's book, *Silent Spring*,[9] published in 1962, raised a cry about the toxic effects of chemicals used in agriculture. A host of other studies have followed and have raised the ecological consciousness of people around the world. Many thoughtful people are now convinced that human beings must now function as a creative element in the living cell and not like unstable adolescents, destroying things before they understand their true value. It is essential for the well-being of planet Earth that we give up our exploitative ways and move into a more ecologically harmonious relationship with the Earth. If we do not do this in an effective and comprehensive way, the Earth community will be in dire straits within a few decades. What is taking place today in Ethiopia, the Sudan and other countries of North Africa will be commonplace for over a thousand million people, and countless life-forms in the Earth community will simply vanish.

It might be good to stop here and try to discern some of the principles which seem to be guiding the cosmic story. If such principles are evident and if they have been operative from the beginning, right through each phase of the story of the universe, then it would be wise for the human actors within the story to respect these principles in all their activity.

When we look at the various phases of the story of the universe from the original homogeneous 'stuff', through the transformations which took place in the core of the stars, to the fashioning of the Earth as a planet hospitable to life, we are stuck by the fact that the urge to produce many and varied beings is the primary urge of the emergent story. We see it in the original transformations of the undifferentiated 'stuff' of the fireball. It is evident in the transformations which took place in the heart of the supernovas. We see it in bowels of the Earth in the different crystalline structures of minerals, rock formations, and stupendous and bewildering variety of non-living and living beings. We see it in the diversity, symbiosis and flexibility of a healthy ecosystem. It leaves its signature in the wide variety of cultures, settlement patterns, social, economic, political and religious systems across the human spectrum. The story would stagnate and fall back under its own weight if the urge to diversify was not bursting out at every crevice.

It would seem to make sense if human activity respected this diversity. Unfortunately as we have seen, the assembly-line, mass-production processes of recent technology do not value diversity. Standardization, interchangeability of parts, efficiency and productivity are much more highly prized. The urge to standardize, rather than cultivate diversity, is particularly destructive and tragic when naturally diverse and sturdy ecosystems like tropical forests are destroyed and are replaced with monocrop-plantation agriculture. The parasitic-al nature of this kind of industrial agriculture is very evident in Mindanao, where multinational agribusinesses Stanfilco, Del Monte and United Fruit run large fruit plantations. Even in the short term the operation can only be effective if increasing quantities of chemicals are used. In the long term, of course, it has no future because erosion and the massive use of chemicals will wash away the soil and destroy its fertility.

The destructive impact of forty years of growing sugar on the island of Negros in the Philippines is summed up very well by McCoy in *Priests on Trial*:[10] 'The region has experienced a net economic regression, moving from an integrated indust-rial-subsistence economy that could feed and clothe itself to a dependence on monocrop sugar production marked by mass poverty and periodic starvation.'

As I am writing this chapter the local papers are full of accounts of poverty and mass starvation in Negros. Some feel that the fortunes of the people will rise again if the price of sugar improves, but the history of the past forty years reveals otherwise. It also bears out the wisdom of the Earth: diversity at all levels, including economics, is essential for vitality and life.

Revealing the 'Withinness' of Things'

Coupled with an increased diversity, as the story progresses, and intimately linked to it, one finds, according to Teilhard, an expanding consciousness and an ever-increasing interiority. Each reality has its own intelligibility or interiority. It carries within itself a unique manifestation of the ultimate mystery of life. Understood in this way, each reality in the story, from the hydrogen atom on, has its own unique value, irrespective of its usefulness to human beings, and as such it must be respected. It goes without saying that human beings manifest the numinous presence in a more complete way than the hydrogen atom. Nevertheless, the dual dimension is present from the beginning. The story of the universe, or cosmogenesis, as Teilhard calls it, has a double thrust – increased 'complexification' and expanding consciousness. We return to a familiar theme of the story. Any mechanistic approach to the universe, which merely articulates the physical dimension, is radically defective and dangerous when it becomes the basis of human activity.

The Cosmos is, in fact, a geophysical and biospiritual reality to which human beings must learn to relate in its totality. The numinous dimension of all reality—which must become the foundation of any ecologically-based spirituality—is best experienced through symbols. Our analytical faculties tend to dissect and fragment things. Where the conceptual world often divides realities from each other, symbols are connective. Meanings reflect and reverberate off each other, mutually reinforcing and deepening our insight into the meaning of things. A renewed experience of natural symbols, of Water, Earth, Fire, Wind and Life-Forms, can serve as a salutary antidote to the excessive analysis, rationalization and fragmentation of our mechanically-oriented world. Through symbols we experience the Earth in a holistic and creative way which emphasizes human and Earth interrelatedness. In this way we can get beyond the barriers which our artificially constructed world often places between us and the natural world. Carried along by this stream of thought, human beings reach their full stature in relation to the entire cosmic process. Because we are the conscious dimension of the universe, our primary vocation is to recognize and celebrate the beauty and wonder of this magnificent creation.

Diversity and 'withinness' are not the final words in the story of the Cosmos, according to Teilhard. There is a comprehensive interdependence and communion which binds all reality and every phase of the story together. The laws of gravity tie every particle in the universe to every other particle in an unbreakable bond. This bonding increases its complexity as one crosses from non-living to living beings. The laws governing the biological and genetic unity of the living are articulated in both Darwin's and Mendel's work. This affinity of being for being is a property of all life, as Teilhard stresses. If there were no pressure for simple molecules to unite, 'it would be impossible for love to appear higher up with us, in hominized form'. Love is the highest expression of this communion. It embraces the natural world, fellow human beings and ultimately God. The transformative power of love is now pushing human consciousness to reach up and achieve a new level of union at Omega point. The communion and love that binds all reality together reminds us that all living forms are, in reality, members of one large family, so that in a very real way we are brothers, sisters and cousins.

The above framework which emerges from Teilhard's vision could form the scaffolding for a universal story of creation as we move towards the twenty-first century. The story, at least in its physical articulation, is now being told wherever modern sciences are taught in schools – in Africa, India, China, the USSR, Oceania and in both North and South America. As the elements of the story are now widespread, it could become a unifying force for the total Earth community in the not-too-distant future. In order to capture people's imagination, the story will need to be told not just in the abstract form of scientific language, but it will have to be sung, set to music and painted in such a way that its beauty and grandeur can lure us away from the life-destroying story that now grips us.

While it is a universal story, it has nothing of the levelling quality of modern technology. The story will have a different flavour in different regions and cultures of the Earth. Those who tell it in a desert will have quite a different saga from those who tell it in the midst of the lush growth of the tropical rain forest. In each individual setting the story will celebrate the emergence of the Earth, that particular bio-region with all its richness, and the heritages of the people who are both shaped by the land and shape it.

The story of the coming into being of the Philippines – an archipelago in a tropical zone at the meeting point between two of the Earth's plates, surrounded by a ring of volcanoes and constantly being jolted by earthquakes – is of particular interest to all Filipinos. The life-story includes the emergence of the tropical forests, the mangrove swamps and the coral reefs. The human side of the Filipino story has its unique dimension, beginning with the Negritos who first came to these islands and who are still found on the islands of Luzon and Mindanao. These were followed by wave after wave of Malay peoples. The Philippines is strategically located, and historically it has been a point of confluence for many of the major civilizations.

Some scholars maintain that the Philippines came under the influence of the Indic world during the height of the Nadjapahit empire.[11] Chinese traders have been visiting the Philippines for 2,000 years, and permanent Chinese settlements were established soon after the arrival of the Spanish. Islam has also shaped the Philippines' story since the fifteenth century, as have Christianity and western culture in both the Spanish and American colonial periods. Relations between all these influences have not always been harmonious, as anyone familiar with Philippine history and the current situation knows, but this unique blend opens up enormous creative possibilities. Now that we are starting to think of the Earth as a single community, Filipino education must impart every aspect of this story. Only by knowing the story will Filipinos really see the richness of the tropical forest, the mangrove swamps and the coral reefs, and the unique heritage which is theirs. Knowing the story will empower them to cherish their land and culture and to do something to save them before it is too late.

The Irish story too has its own beauty. Poets and storytellers in Ireland have, over the centuries, spoken of ancient Ireland. Little did they know that the rock saucer underpinning the

island goes back an incredible two billion years. These rocks
can be seen in parts of Donegal and Kilmore Quay in County
Wexford. Many strands are woven into the tapestry of the
Irish story; the long history of the process of rock formation is
itself a wonderful story. There were long moments of quiet,
during which rain and sun gradually wore down mountains.
There were also moments of tension and violent upheaval,
which threw up mountains and spewed out lava in
extraordinary shapes, as one sees when driving along the north
Antrim coast.

The history of life on the island, beginning with the
primitive mosses and lichens, through the giant ferns of the
Carboniferous period and the various ice-ages, adds flesh to
the rocky bones. The Burren country in County Clare is a
living testimony to this unique life-history. There one finds
various species of Arctic, Alpine and Mediterranean plants
living side by side. The story would not be complete without
the human actors in Ireland. The various waves of people who
have come to these shores have all left their mark on the
physical landscape and on the shape of Irish culture. It has its
moments of greatness, beauty and exaltation. There are also
moments of pain, despair, contradiction and desolation. But
every facet of the story is important for any in-depth
understanding of Ireland and the Irish people today. It also
clarifies the options open to the Irish today, building firmly on
all that has gone before instead of wrecking it in a few short
decades.

This very inadequate glance through Filipino and Irish
history is only meant to demonstrate that the story will need to
set down its roots in each bio-region. It will not cast aside the
particular myths of origin or identity of each culture or
religion. Both the Genesis stories will still play an important
role in formulating many of the most important values for
Jews and Christians. Through them many people will still
experience the love of God in creating this beautiful world, the
response this should evoke from human beings, and the norms
which should govern much of human behaviour.

It will, however, mean that the Genesis stories will have to
be understood in a new, wider context. In Genesis, the
physical world is seen as static. There is no co-evolution of

micro and macro systems which together form the cradle for life. We saw many examples of this in our presentation of the story of the universe. The emergence of the first micro-organisms in the original oceans and the atmosphere were a prerequisite for the next stage in the evolution of life.

In each phase of the story of the universe, there is a dynamic interplay between the many forces that carry the story along. It is not static or unchanging, but constantly being transformed in an emergent process. In Genesis, and most of the traditional myths of origin of the universe, the stars, the sun, the moon and the Earth itself are put there in a single action. There is no vision of them emerging as such. Usually they are there as a backdrop against which the human actors work out their personal or cultural destiny. These stories now need to be placed within the context of the emerging universe, where everything is vitally related to everything else. The myths of particular cultures and religions – the *Vedas* in India, the *Tudbulul* among the T'boli – will take on new significance within the context of this story of the universe. The local articulation of the story will celebrate the diversity of many cultures and peoples, the unique identity of each people and the communion of the human and the universe community.

Like any functional, vital myth, the new story of the universe gives deeper meaning to our lives and evokes from us a commitment to organize our world according to its insights. It can guide, encourage and nourish us as we abandon the exploitative world of the recent past and set about building a sustainable world where there is equality and sufficiency for all. The story should help us see the true significance of the loss of the tropical forests. The countless life-forms in that particular ecosystem encode about 300 million years of the Earth's history. The story points out the sheer madness of eliminating this particular habitat within a generation or two, no matter how attractive the immediate economic gains might appear to be.

It raises profoundly disturbing questions about many aspects of modern culture which are inconsistent with the needs of the various life-systems. Many of our modern technologies are cumulatively weakening the fabric of life. Nuclear technology is probably the most visible one. There is danger of atomic radiation at every stage of the nuclear process, beginning with the mining itself. Accidents like those at the Three Mile Island nuclear plant in Pennsylvania and at Chernobyl in the Ukraine remind us how fragile nuclear technology is, how fallible the human beings who operate it are and how lax monitoring agencies can be in enforcing safety requirements. If accidents like this can happen in the USA and the USSR where there are many trained scientists and technicians to operate the nuclear plants, one fears for the worst when a host of nuclear plants, like the one in Bataan in the Philippines, begin to operate in the Third World countries. To add to the possibility of human error, the Bataan nuclear plant is located less than a hundred miles from five volcanoes, four of which are considered active.

Once the nuclear genie is let out of the bottle it will haunt the Earth community for thousands of years. It would seem irresponsible to develop nuclear power in an extensive way when no safe method has yet been found for storing and disposing of nuclear waste. E.F. Schumacher, the author of *Small is Beautiful*, maintains that 'no place on Earth can be shown to be safe, for disposing of nuclear waste'.[12] We pointed out in chapter 3 that much nuclear waste today is dumped in the deepest parts of the oceans on the false assumption that no life exists there. Recent deep-sea exploration has discovered life-forms in every part of the ocean. Once the radioactive material is absorbed into the biological cycle it contaminates everything – water, plankton, algae and fish. Higher life forms that feed on these have the capacity to concentrate the radioactivity by a factor of 1,000 or more.

We are now accumulating huge quantities of high level nuclear waste. The present nuclear plants in the United States will have 200 million gallons on hand by the year 2000. It will take much of this material between 800 to 1,000 years to decay to what is at present thought to be a harmless level. The half life of plutonium 293 which is produced by every nuclear reactor is 240,000 years. So by developing this technology we are placing every generation to follow us at risk.

While challenging our technology and encouraging us to adopt a new life-style is important, the central task of the new story in the immediate future is to help us redefine what it means to be human. The story of the universe will no longer allow us to place an almost unbridgeable chasm between the human and the natural world which has facilitated our exploitation of the latter, especially in recent centuries. Unless we do this quickly we will destroy the very world that supports us.

Yet the human imperial stance towards the natural world runs very deep and is very extensive. A good example of this came to light during a seminar on Ecology and Social Justice held at the Asian Social Institute in Manila in August 1984. The organizers of the seminar invited representatives from a fishermen's co-operative located at Lake Laguna to address the participants about the effects of industrial pollution on their lives. Laguna de Bay, as it is known, is the largest and, until recently, the most productive lake in the Philippines. It comprises around 90,000 hectares and has a shoreline of 220 kilometres. The fishermen presented a litany of wanton destruction to this once beautiful lake which older people in the area called 'mala-paraiso' (semi-paradise). The fishermen described in detail how this 'paradise' has been lost in recent decades: loggers on near-by hills have significantly reduced the level of the lake; industrial effluent from numerous industries on the shores of the lake and sewage from nearby towns often turn the water into sludge. Naturally the fishermen's catch has dwindled and so they and their families have become increasingly impoverished. They complained that since their livelihood has been destroyed they have no money to buy food, clothing or medicine. The final straw is that they cannot even find work in the local factories which have polluted their lake.

As I listened, I felt that it was particularly tragic that the fishermen, whose lives had been ruined by ecological destruction, had themselves internalized and accepted the values of a money economy. Their loss, after all, went far beyond their inability to generate money to buy food or other goods. In a real way they had lost their primary source of food, not just the cash to buy goods in the local supermarket. They had also lost their source of health which primarily comes from good nutritious food and a healthy environment. It is almost certain that the processed food which they buy in the store is nowhere as nutritious as their natural source of food. Their emotional life was also impoverished, as they had lost a source for song and poetic inspiration. No one in the future will sing a joyful song about the cesspool that is the Pasig River as it flows through Manila. Finally, their spiritual life is also stunted. Fishermen in seaside towns here in Mindanao have often told me that it is during the long hours that they spend in their boats, especially on a starry night, that they experience the presence of the Divine most intimately.

The solution to the fishermen's problems is not to build more factories where they can get jobs and a weekly paycheck, but to regenerate their lakes. This means taking care of the water, the aquatic plant life and all the varieties of fish and marine life in the lake. If this ecosystem can ever be restored to anything like its former splendour, the worries of the fishermen will diminish substantially. In an abundant environment, human beings normally have the ingenuity to look after themselves. In other words, real, lasting development for the fishermen of Lake Laguna involves caring for the life of the lake.

This story tells us that human beings must find once again their proper context in the natural world. To focus merely on the human segment of the story and pretend that we have no organic connection with the rest of creation is to overlook the greater part of the twenty billion years of the story of the universe. In recent centuries human beings have not been at ease in the natural world. Our scientific, humanist and religious traditions have shown a considerable antagonism towards the natural world and have attempted to create the illusion that we are not a part of nature.

The process has intensified since the beginning of the industrial age. Until this time the vast majority of human beings were in constant, often daily, contact with the Earth. The fishermen, farmers or shepherds would not survive long if they decided to repudiate their dependence on nature. The industrial age has created the illusion that at last the shackles tying the human to the natural world have been severed and that humans have been liberated. Our food no longer comes from our own farm or garden, but in plastic containers from the shelves of the nearest supermarket. Modern city life with its highways, subways, communications network and factory life almost succeeds in cutting us off completely from nature. Today we must consciously work to break through this man-made mesh and re-establish our rightful place in the Earth community.

Finally, the reinsertion of the human into the natural world does not in any way belittle or downgrade human consciousness. On the contrary, as we have seen in Teilhard, it gives new breadth and depth to the human venture as it roots us very definitely at the origins of all reality. We are reconnected in a creative way with every other entity in the universe in a way that will allow us to assume a new creative role in the process. Our human vocation is not to despoil, plunder and pillage, but to foster, nurture, bless and give thanks. This sense of vocation emerges from our growing realization that human beings and the rest of creation grow together and share a common destiny.

PART TWO

A CALL TO A NEW THEOLOGY

6

A THEOLOGY OF CREATION IN THE LIGHT OF THE NEW STORY

Part 1 of this book argued that the rapid deterioration of the natural environment, which provides the support system for all life on Earth, is the most serious problem of our times. I presented data from current research on the condition of air, soil, forests, living forms and water, with special emphasis on the situation in the Philippines and in Ireland. I maintained that much of the destruction stems from the processes of modern technology. The benefits which people in industrialized countries have reaped from technology have prevented us from assessing its full cost, especially to other members of the Earth community. I presented a brief history of the origins and rise of the machine age and in Chapter 5 I attempted to seek a new path for humans to relate to the Earth in a way that will be mutually enhancing and sustaining.

The effort to reinsert and locate the human within the Earth community spills over into any systematic reflection of the experience of Christian faith or theology. We might begin our discussion in Part 2 with Thomas Berry's blunt statement that the serious ecological devastation which I have described is endangering the future of the Earth and so poses a very serious problem for all religious faiths, including the Christian faith. This challenge, one of the most crucial in the history of the Earth, should spur Christian thinkers to fashion a new theology of creation adequate for today's task. The sad fact is, as many commentators point out, that up to this moment the

Catholic Church's voice on the ecological crisis has been muted. In many ways the Church seems unaware of what is happening or too preoccupied with many other problems.

While everyone – Church people, the wider human community and all the community of the living – will pay dearly for this failure to respond adequately to the pain of the Earth, yet the failure is understandable in the light of the demise of the old 'Christian' cosmology which I traced in Chapter 4. The framework for relating to the natural world collapsed, leaving Christians adrift. In the wake of this collapse, Catholic theological and spiritual traditions abandoned any real wrestling with the mystery of creation. Theologians focused exclusively on human history. In this way, as we have seen, they abandoned to others speculation about the natural world. Even then their perspective on human history, drawn almost exclusively from the Augustinian tradition of Fall and Redemption, was one-sided.

The move away from a creation-centred theology did not end there. Despite the article of the Creed affirming the Resurrection of the body, the understanding of salvation tended to reject the world of nature and concentrate on redeeming people, and very often just the soul, *from* the natural world. Given this dualistic approach to reality with its preference for the spiritual, the theology of creation, even that based on an inadequate cosmology, receded until it almost disappeared from manuals of theology and seminary formation programmes. The rich creation tradition of Genesis, Second Isaiah, the Psalms and the Wisdom literature in the Old Testament was forgotten. So too the creation dimension of Jesus's teaching was overlooked along with the holistic creation theology of Paul, Benedict, Francis, Hildegarde of Bingen, Meister Eckhart and Thomas Aquinas in the exclusive concentration on human salvation in a world beyond the present. Only in the past thirty years, due mainly to the impetus which Teilhard's writings have given to the Christian world, have theologians once again begun to search for and discover a new theology of creation. They are drawing their inspiration from a creative dialogue with scientists, other religious traditions and the depths of the Judeo-Christian faith.

An Attitude to God

We might begin reflections on a theology of creation by asking what is the effect of the new story on our idea of God. This is the crucial question because our understanding of the Earth rests upon our attitude towards God. As we begin our search for an adequate understanding of God for our era we must of course look at the assumptions we bring with us, because these will in large measure determine how we view the Divine. Bacon, Descartes and Newton were not irreligious men. Yet it was their inadequate emphasis on the spiritual dimension that set the stage for the machine age.

Historians of religion and comparative religion scholars tell us that, across the human spectrum in time and space, there are very different and sometimes contradictory understandings of the experience of the Divine presence. In many tribal societies, the Divine is often seen as a pervasive, diffuse spirit presence throughout the Cosmos, the Earth and natural phenomena. In a particular way the Divine manifests itself in natural phenomena – trees, rocks, rivers, mountains, volcanoes and the like.

This approach to the world of the numinous is very common throughout Southeast Asia. Among the T'boli in the Philippines, for example, each river, tree or mountain has its own spirit. Much of the religious ritual is geared to pleasing or appeasing the spirits. The people are intent on attracting the blessings of the good spirits and warding off destruction from evil spirits. Cosmic phenomena like eclipses, and natural destructive phenomena like earthquakes and typhoons, are given a moral meaning. They are often seen as punishment for encroaching on the domain of the spirits by altering the natural world in a significant way. Even the very simple matter of cutting down a tree or building a house demands the appropriate rituals to recognize the rights of the spirit world.

This approach to the numinous world is also holistic. There is no cutting off of the human from the natural world. Nature is not seen as raw material for human consumption to be manipulated in whatever way people choose. Rather it is filled with spirit presence and as such must be respected. As we will see, there is much that Christians can learn from the approach of tribal religions which might prevent us abusing the natural world. Tribal people are sensitive to spirit presence in the world around them.

Many of the great classical religions swing to the other extreme. The Greek philosophical tradition draws off all spirit presence from the phenomenal world and condenses it into a notion of the Divine which is seen as transcendent. In contrast to the phenomenal world which is constantly changing, the Divine is seen as static and timeless, beyond the corruption of the world. This perfect, unchanging Divine person is not intimately involved in the joys and pains of the Earth community. He is beyond it all and not passionately caught up in its destiny.

With this approach, important links in the chain connecting all reality were broken. The break was widened further by the mechanistic assumptions which have crept into our under-standing of God since the beginning of the machine age. The Cosmos, as we have seen, is viewed as an exquisitely constructed clock with all the parts functioning perfectly. Against this background God is seen as the omnipotent clock-maker who has fashioned the Cosmos, wound up the clock, and more or less abandoned it to its own devices. Since the whole process is basically static, God is seen to have little concern for it. Unfortunately this vision is one of the sources from which the contemporary Christian notion of God is formed. It is particularly destructive of the Earth, because, if God is thought of as not being concerned about what is happening to creation, why should human beings worry unduly?

The second source for our understanding of God is of course the biblical tradition. Yahweh, the God of Israel, is faithful both to his people and to his creation (Gen. 8:22 and 9:9, 10, 13). The sequence of day and night and seasonal variations are interpreted as expressions of his commitment to the Earth community. His concern is personal and active rather than merely as a primary cause. Psalm 104:27 pictures all the creatures looking to God 'to give them their food in due time'.

So while it is true that the biblical understanding of God does include a sense of his immanence in the natural world, nevertheless, it must be recognized that this is not the most important concern for the biblical tradition. While tribal religion emphasizes the continuity between the phenomenal world and the spirit world, there seems to be a great need to differentiate the Divine and the human from the natural world in the Bible. According to Phyllis Bird,[1] the primary assertion in the first – priestly – account of creation, 'God created mankind in his own image and likeness', is that both God and human beings are distinguished from the natural world. This is further emphasized by the fact that the creative act emerges from God's word and is not mediated through any earthly medium, like the potter's clay in the second account of creation. Furthermore, any representation of the Divine is strictly prohibited (Deut. 4:15–40), lest people forget that the Divine is infinitely removed from natural phenomena such as the sun and the moon and particularly the cycles of nature.

Frederick Turner, in *Beyond Geography*,[2] argues that environmental factors are responsible for this cleavage. In the barren, inhospitable environment of the Middle East, both the pastoralists and early settlers in the area felt the need to separate the Divine and the human from the natural world. In order to survive in the sparse mountains, barren deserts, steppes and narrow plains, human beings had to channel all their efforts into dominating, controlling and taming the natural world. Even in an area like the Fertile Crescent, countless generations had to wrestle with nature by draining swamps, designing irrigation canals and terracing hillsides in order that the natural world might be productive and support the emerging civilization. When compared to the lush, abundant vegetation of the tropics, or even the fruitfulness of the temperate zones in Europe, the land in the Middle East was harsh, stubborn and not very fruitful.

There was also need for constant vigilance. Unless human beings continued to battle against the elements there was always a dread that the wilderness would in a very short time over-run what man had so laboriously conquered. Vestiges of this need constantly to push back the chaos are present in the thrust to separate the light from the darkness and the waters below from the waters above in Gen. 1:3–8. Only through the constant toil of building and clearing the irrigation ditches, planting vineyards, and rotating crops and pasture lands could the wilderness be kept in check. This is reflected in the punishment meted out to Adam in Gen. 3:17–20.

> Because you have listened to your wife
> and have eaten from the tree which I forbade you,
> accursed shall be the ground on your account.
> With labour you shall win your food from it
> all the days of your life.
> It will grow thorns and thistles for you,
> none but wild plants for you to eat.
> You shall gain your bread by the sweat of your brow
> until you return to the ground.

This does recognize that the Earth is the source of life, but it is not a benign, abundant Earth, like a tropical island that with little or no human effort provides sufficient food for both individuals and a society. It is an antagonistic world that constantly needs to be broken by the plough and transformed by the sweat of human labour.

The constant watchfulness needed to keep the wilderness at bay is seen most clearly in the cities that gradually grew up in the Middle East in the second and first millenia before Christ. The wall, the gardens and the granary were important symbols of human beings' constant battle against the elements. The thick sturdy walls insulated people from the buffeting of nature, and the attack of enemies. Inside the walls they felt secure and in control, and could fashion their own world. Outside the walls the wild, unpredictable and dangerous wilderness began. Even with heroic courage, human beings could never completely domesticate it. They must be always alert; nature could never be completely trusted.

The communal granary was also another important symbol of the city as it provided another kind of security. By producing extra grain and storing it, human beings were no longer dependent on the whims of nature. They could begin to plan and organize for the future.

Finally, in the cultivated space within the city walls called gardens, human beings could dominate nature completely. Here they could take delight in nature in full knowledge that they were the masters and that nature had been shorn of its fearful, awesome and unpredictable aspect. The garden image, as we will see, plays an important part in the biblical notion of creation.

The human environment, no less than the physical environment, played an important role in shaping the biblical understanding of the Divine. The contours of the biblical message about God and the Earth were worked out in Israel in opposition to the fertility cults practised by the Canaanites. We see from the constant railing of the prophets against going up to 'the high places' that these fertility rites proved seductive to the Israelites when they abandoned their nomadic ways and began to settle in the land, plant crops and tend vines.

The Canaanite religion had much in common with the tribal religions discussed above. The Divine reality revealed itself in the rhythms of the natural world, especially the mystery of fertility. There were both male and female principles within the divine reality itself. The joining of these two principles in the mating of the gods and goddesses ensured the fertility of crops, flocks and the human community. The fertility rituals practised by the Canaanites included ritual prostitution. The ritual intercourse between the suppliant and the temple prostitutes invited the gods and goddesses to do likewise so that the human community would experience the blessings of a bountiful harvest. In the final analysis the ceremony was seen to ensure the continuation of the fertility cycle and re-establish cosmic order.

Israel, on the other hand, saw the divine power revealed primarily in concrete historical events. Yahweh was seen primarily not so much as creator of the world as the God who liberated Israel from slavery in Egypt (Ex. 3), and moulded them as a people (Deut. 32:63). The belief in Yahweh as creator did not emerge until later. The dominant Exodus event was sealed and celebrated in a once-for-all covenant which linked Yahweh and the people of Israel in an unbreakable bond and formed the basis for a continuing relationship.

The demands of the covenant confronted every Israelite. Not even a famous king like David could disregard the demands of the covenant, as we see in the confrontation between David and Nathan in 2 Samuel 12:1–14. The central feasts and rituals of Israel celebrated historical events rather than the rhythms of nature. Feasts like the Passover and Unleavened Bread, which originally were agricultural festivals based on the sequences of nature, were, in the light of the Exodus, transformed into an historical commemoration of Yahweh's intervention on behalf of his people. In this religious milieu, ritual was not seen as technology for cajoling, controlling or placating the gods, but as events recalling God's intervention in human history and his challenging the people to build a just human community.

Masculine and Feminine in God

Christian writers in the feminist movement call attention today to another important legacy of the biblical tradition for our notion of God which has important ramifications for our growing ecological awareness. Probably because of the polemic against the feminine element in the Canaanite cult, biblical religion tends to be patriarchal and hierarchical. Both the dominant streams in the Bible and later Christian writers have emphasized, often in a way that women find oppressive and alienating, the masculine image of God. Both traditions use the masculine pronoun when referring to God in their liturgies and devotional literature. The masculine face of God is further accentuated by the masculine attributes which are commonly attributed to God. Yahweh fights on Israel's behalf, he leads the Israelites through the desert to freedom and a new land. He is spoken of as king, shepherd, redeemer, judge and father.

To avoid any misunderstanding of what I am saying here, my reference to masculine or feminine qualities does not mean that these qualities are always clearly defined and that they are biologically determined. Neither am I overlooking the insights of Jungian psychology which sees a masculine and feminine dimension in each human personality. All I am saying is that in particular cultures, in this case the ancient Hebrew, Greek, Roman and modern western cultures, certain roles and distinctive behavioural patterns are commonly attributed to men or women on the basis of sex difference. Many roles which are specifically masculine are attributed to God.

To further exacerbate the anti-feminine bias, the biblical culture in general ascribed an inferior role to women. This was particularly heightened after the Exile. Only two roles were open to women – wife and mother. They were not allowed to assume any political or religious office and had no legal standing apart from their relationship with their fathers or husbands. The oppressed and unenviable position of women is captured in a morning prayer from the inter-testamental period. In this prayer the pious Jewish male blessed and thanked God that 'he was neither a Gentile, a woman or a slave'.

Even a cursory reading of the New Testament reveals that Jesus' attitude and behaviour towards women marked a radical break with the tradition of the later Old Testament times. Jesus broke many of the taboos which were based on sexual discrimination. His attitude towards the Samaritan woman in John 4:7–42 is a striking example. Speaking to a strange Samaritan woman was taboo, so the disciples were shocked when they found Jesus teaching her (John 4:27). But the most amazing thing of all in a society in which women's behaviour was circumscribed, is that Jesus allowed her to witness to him in her own community (John 4:39). In other situations in the New Testament we find that he was not prevented from carrying out his mission by so-called ritual taboos. He attended to the woman with an issue of blood without any embarrassment (Luke 8:43–8).

It is tragic for women themselves, for the Church and for the wider Earth community, that during the greater part of the Christian era the dominant spiritual tradition in the Church failed to follow this creative lead of Jesus. From the early patristic period the Church, taking its cue from the milieu in which it lived, rather than the Gospel of Jesus, slipped back into an Old Testament attitude towards women. It effectively denied them any official role in the Church. The two most influential thinkers in the history of the Church – St Augustine and St Thomas Aquinas – subscribed to the view that women were inferior to men and that they needed to be protected.

This question of gender in God is vitally linked to the wider theme of our Christian stance towards the natural world. Feminist historians rightly point out that the language and mentality which over the centuries has oppressed women and brutalized men also went hand in hand with man's efforts to dominate, subdue and ultimately despoil the natural world. The male 'macho' image in many cultures was sharpened through man's strivings to dominate women and the Earth.

It is important therefore to search out other strands in our God-Talk that are more sensitive to the feminine dimension of God. The French theologian Yves Congar in an article 'The Spirit as God's Femininity'[3] locates this tradition in some of the prophets and especially in the Wisdom literature.

God's compassion is beautifully and tenderly present in a number of well-known texts. Hosea in a very moving passage describes God's abiding love for Israel despite her unfaithfulness (Hos. 11:1–11). Isaiah asks in chapter 49:15: 'Can a woman forget her sucking child that she should have no compassion on the son of her womb?' The language here is decidedly feminine. Linguistic evidence confirms this. In Hebrew the word for compassion, *râham*, is the plural form of the word *rehem*, which means womb.

Congar argues that the Wisdom literature describes the Spirit of God as feminine. A few texts will suffice to catch this flavour. In Sir. 14:22, wisdom is courted like a young maiden. In an earlier text in the same book, 5:2–8, she appears as a caring mother and a provident wife. In the Book of Wisdom, 7:7–18, she is prized above all other good things 'as the mother of all humanity' (Wis. 7:12).

Wisdom is seen as the source of creativity; Wisdom 8:1 sees wisdom as 'ordering all things.' This takes up the theme already present in Gen. 1:2, and identifies wisdom with the creative Spirit that hovers over the waters and brings forth the cosmos and all life from the chaos. A similar image of gestation is evoked by Luke's account of the conception of Jesus (Luke 1:35). This maternal, moulding role of the Spirit is also to the fore in the Baptism account in the synoptic gospels (Luke 3:22, Mark 1:10, Matt. 3:16). The Spirit descends upon Jesus to prepare and strengthen him for his messianic mission. Paul speaks of the decisive role of the Spirit in the Resurrection and glorification of Jesus (Rom. 1:4). In Acts 2:1–13, the enlivening and empowering role of the Spirit is the decisive event responsible for releasing the creativity of the infant Church on Pentecost day. In the power of the Spirit, the Apostles bear testimony to Jesus and continue his work.

From this brief summary we can see that in the biblical tradition the feminine dimension of God is most evident in the Wisdom tradition. In the New Testament this tradition blossoms into the theology of the Spirit of God. So even from within our own tradition the over-emphasis on the masculine in God can now be balanced by a strong feminine presence. The emergence of the feminist and ecological movements at much the same time challenges us to ponder more deeply our own tradition, and delight in the discovery of riches we never dreamt existed. This new holistic view of God as Father and Mother invites us to shun any ideological understanding of human–Earth relations which refuses to take into account the interdependence of all living and non-living beings. This discovery of a feminine dimension in God should increase our sensitivity to her/his presence in the world that he/she created in love as the flowering planet of the universe.

God in Creation

The final shape of the Christian belief in the Divine is to see the mystery of God as expressed in neither singularity nor plurality but as Trinity. So even in the heart of the mystery of Being itself we have the threefold dynamic which is, as we saw on pages 93-96, operative in the story of the emergent universe.[4]

The first principle of expressive Being which we identify with the Father is the urge to create. This outpouring surge of energy manifests itself in our highly differentiated universe with its galaxies, vast interstellar space, the solar system and the profusion of life on Earth, all finely tuned into one living community. The first article of the Creed affirms that God the Father almighty is 'the creator of heaven and Earth'. The Divine power and providence guided this stupendous process, particularly at those moments which are crucial for the entire process. Some of these moments would include the origin event when, as we mentioned on page 83, the universe could have exploded or collapsed back on itself, the birth of the solar system, and the positioning of the sun and the Earth in such a way that together they could eventually support and nourish life. Finally, the transition from non-human to human life is a high point for the whole process and gives it all a new meaning.

At these and many other 'fragile' moments when the whole evolutionary process could easily have been derailed, there must have been a special intensity in the divine guidance which both envelops the creation and is present at its very core. Considering everything we have said so far about the present threat to the life-systems of the Earth it is clear that we are living today through another crucial phase, not just for humans, but also for the total evolutionary process. In this moment of history we are becoming more and more aware that much of the guidance for all the Earth is now in the hands of human beings. The birth of the world-wide ecological movement which is dedicated to establishing in an effective way a new creative human–Earth relationship is surely an indication that God is still guiding creation even after 20,000,000,000 years.

The second principle to emerge from the story is the 'withinness' dimension of all reality, beginning with the fireball. Each reality in the universe has its own inner radiance, which points to and reflects the ultimate mystery of God. Christians believe that Christ is the ultimate revelation of the Father. The mystery of the Incarnation as it is proclaimed in John 1:14 consists of the revelation that God, in Jesus, identified himself totally with the human, and thereby with all creation. In Christ, God wedded himself in an irreversible way to the totality of the emergent creation. If the story of the universe tells us that each individual human being is in a real way co-extensive with the total story, then most certainly Christ is co-extensive with, and a central dimension of every reality. He carries within himself the signature of the supernovas and the geology and life history of the Earth.

If, for example, flowering trees and shrubs had not appeared 300 million years ago, then mammalian life would not have followed. Without that concentration of nutrients no

human being, including Christ, would ever have walked on
Earth. So that particular memory and every other memory of
the emergent process is carried within the Christ reality. In
him all things are united. Paul summarizes this by saying that
'he is all and in all' (Col. 3:11). Paul had no idea of an
emergent universe, but his insight into the cosmic dimension
of Christ captures accurately the reality of things. The
doctrine of the Incarnation, rightly understood, is an
invitation to all peoples to love and cherish the Earth and to
find the Divine therein. If this sensitivity to the Christ reality
in all beings were to become widespread among Christians, we
would once again, as a people, recapture the reverence and
respect for nature which one finds in many tribal societies.
The respect would not be based on fear but on the
fundamental, organic unity of all things in Christ. This is the
theme of one of the final blessings at the Catholic Vigil Mass
on Christmas night: 'When the Word became man, Earth was
joined to heaven. May he give you his peace and goodwill, and
fellowship with all the heavenly host.' A pity they did not add
"earthly" as well; that would have been more in keeping with
the mystery of the Incarnation.

In Christ, the outpouring love of the Father for creation is
experienced in a special way in the Cross. Christ is the
powerless, crucified God who in his own person is rent
asunder by the mystery of evil. The God he reveals to us is not
some immutable, primary cause beyond the flux of the Earth
and unmoved by suffering and pain. He is God who is
passionately involved in his creation and wishes to see it
flowering.

Finally there is the feminine dimension of God which we
identify with the Holy Spirit. She is the principle of
communion, binding all reality together. The Holy Spirit is
the source of all unity. All attraction, all bonding, all intimacy
and communion flows from the Spirit. Each of these
relationships is sacred to the Spirit. In her the whole universe
is linked together in one nurturing, enveloping embrace. She
is the one who inspires all fruitfulness and creativity – which
are the signs of true bonding and intimacy. From her comes
the great urge to heal what is broken, re-unite what is
separated, and recreate the face of the Earth.

In this section I have attempted to look at our own religious tradition in order to discover the hidden riches which may help us to fashion an appropriate theology of creation for today. Because the biblical tradition is so rich I have found it a veritable gold-mine for the task which I have set myself in this book.

It is important to remember our introductory discussion about the emergence of a sense of the Divine in Israel. In the milieu in which Israel was born, the Divine presence in historical events took precedence over the experience of God in nature. In wrestling with its environment and the historical challenge that it faced, Israel articulated its understanding of the Divine as personal, monotheistic, transcendent, yet intimately involved in the events of history. The gains from this rich interplay were vital to Israel's survival as a nation as she attempted to set down deep roots in the land of Canaan and adjusted herself to the turbulent political realities of the ancient Near East. It fixed a wonderful sense of the Divine which facilitated a very special and intimate relationship between the human and the Divine, and held humans responsible particularly for their behaviour towards each other. It inspired Israel to attempt to weld together a community where peace and justice might reign. Not only the Jewish people and Christians, but the total human community, is indebted to Israel for shaping this vision of the Divine.

With every gain there are losses. This vision of the Divine tends to make people whose lives are shaped by it less sensitive to the presence of God in the sky, the wild flowers, the mountains, the seas, the sun, the moon, the stars, the birds, the trees and all the living creatures of the Earth. It must be remembered, however, that this conception of the Divine was shaped at a time when there was little danger to the Earth community, so the gains far outweighed the losses. But today, with destruction of ecosystems all over the world, our dulled sensitivity to the Divine presence in nature is tragic. And yet as we saw in our discussion of the feminine in God, there are rich nuggets in our religious tradition that are only now coming to light. In order to be creatively relevant to the needs of today we must cherish these insights and allow our religious imagination and emotions to be gripped by the overpowering presence of the Divine in the world around us. Only in this way will we be aroused to work to heal the world before it is completely despoiled.

Keeping in mind the environment out of which the faith of Israel emerged, the first and most important message of the Bible is still that the world was created by a loving personal God (Gen. 1:1). The world does not come from an evil spirit at odds with God, and is not itself evil. As God contemplated his creation he saw 'that it was good' (Gen. 1:13, 18, 21, 26). There is no idea of a dichotomy between matter and spirit which pictures the spirit emanating from a good principle and matter from an evil or corrupting one. The Israelite does not have to retreat from the natural world in order to experience and worship God. Psalm 19:1 states:

The heavens declare the glory of God.
The vault of heaven proclaims His handiwork.
Day discourses of it to day,
night to night hands on the knowledge.

Numerous other texts echo and elaborate on this theme. Some of the more prominent ones are Gen. 10:12-13 and especially Psalm 104, which sings the praises of God the Creator.

Stewardship

God's command to the newly created couple in Genesis 1:28 – 'Be fruitful, multiply, fill the earth and conquer it' – is seen by many commentators as a key text in shaping the human–Earth relationship in the Bible. The above translation is from the Jerusalem Bible. Other translations substitute 'subdue the earth' or 'have domination over it' for 'conquer it'. The injunction makes a lot of sense when understood in the light of the discussion above on the physical environment of the Middle East. Creation itself is seen as bringing order out of chaos – pushing back the wilderness and creating a garden (Gen. 2:8). God himself takes delight in the garden. In Gen. 3:8, he walks in the garden at the time of the evening breeze.

While the harsh environment from which the Bible emerged left its mark in a preference for a tamed environment in which the human was more closely bonded with the Divine than the natural world, this does not mean that the injunction in Genesis can be interpreted as a licence for humans to do what they like with the Earth. The commission is best understood as an invitation to human beings to act as the viceroys of God. Ted F. Peters argues that this is the meaning of the Hebrew word *Radah* used in the text. Like the viceroy of the king, the human being is expected to be just and honest and not to exploit the Earth which God himself experienced as 'very good'.[4] This stewardship pictures human beings in harmony with nature, standing before God and ultimately responsible to God for their management of human affairs and of creation. Even though the human is separated from the rest of creation by being created in God's own image (Gen. 1:27), human dependence on the natural world, and the interdependence of the elements within the natural itself, is not overlooked.

> I give you all plants that bear seed everywhere on earth, and every tree bearing fruit which yields seed: they shall be yours for food. All green plants I give for food to the wild animals, to all the birds of heaven, and reptiles on earth, and every living creature. (Gen. 1:29, 30)

The interdependence of human beings and the rest of the Earth community is further elaborated on in Genesis 8 and 9, especially in the covenant made with Noah after the Flood. It is true that in Genesis 1 and 2 the human is given a special position, but some scripture scholars, like Bernhard Anderson, insist that to focus exclusively on the first two chapters of Genesis and leave chapter 9 out of the reckoning presents a very unbalanced picture of the biblical notion of creation.[5]

One needs to look at the whole saga of creation as it unfolds from chapters 1 to 9. The account begins with the creation of the Heavens, the Earth and all the creatures on Earth, culminating in the human. In chapter 3, sin enters to mar the human–earth and human–divine relationships. The ripples of that original sin stain and distort everything. They fracture family relations with the murder of Abel, and lead to the strange union between the sons of heaven and the daughters of men in chapter 6:2. This cumulative evil precipitated the disaster of the Flood. After the Flood the injunction of Gen. 1:28 is again repeated, but this time in the context of a covenant made, not just with human beings, but with all creation (Gen. 9:8–17).

Anderson sees striking linguistic and thematic correspondence between the Genesis 1 account and Genesis 9.[6] The focus in Genesis 1 is homocentric. In Genesis 9, however, it is centred on all the community of the living: 'This is a sign I am giving for all ages to come, of the covenant between me and you and every living creature with you.' (Gen. 9:12)

This inclusive covenant is at the heart of stewardship. The harmony that should exist between human beings and the natural world emerges from this understanding of inter-dependence. The responsibility is not something that can be taken lightly because, ultimately, the call to stewardship is a privilege bestowed on humankind by God. As with all privileges, human beings will be held accountable for their stewardship. If they are caring and cultivate harmony in all their dealings with each other and the Earth, then they grow in the image and likeness of God.

The demands of stewardship are very clear when it comes to caring for the land which the tribes of Israel occupied. First of all the land is held in common. It is given as a gift in response to the people's fidelity, to their 'obeying my voice and holding fast to my Covenant' (Ex. 19:5). What is given is not outright ownership of the land to use or abuse as one pleases, but rather the right of tenancy. This is so because Yahweh is portrayed as the true landlord, who decrees that 'the land must not be sold in perpetuity, for the land belongs to me and you are only strangers and guests' (Lev. 25:23). Respect for Yahweh's overlordship, care for the land and concern for the less fortunate are all entwined in an earlier injunction in Lev. 25:4–7:

> But in the seventh year, the land is to have a rest, a sabbath for Yahweh. You must not sow your field or prune your vines, or harvest your ungathered corn or gather your grapes from your untrimmed vines. It is to be a year of rest for the land. The sabbath of the land will itself feed you and your servants, men and women, your hired labourer, your guests and all who live with you. For your cattle too and the animals on your land its produce will serve as food.

Incidentally, modern industrial agriculture would do well to recapture this respect for land and allow fields to lie fallow for a period, instead of continually exploiting the resources of the land in order to maximize short-term profits. Wendell Berry in *The Gift of Good Land*[7] concedes that modern farming has had spectacular results in solving the problem of food production. The result, however, is that the 'side effects' threaten the very survival of farming in every country where chemical farming is gaining a footing!

Respect for fowl and domestic animals on which the farmer depends for his livelihood is enjoined in the command, 'You must not muzzle an ox when it is treading out corn' (Deut. 25:4). This respect is further extended to wildlife in Deuteronomy 22:26–27: 'If when out walking, you come across a bird's nest in a tree or in the ground, with chicks or eggs and the mother bird sitting on the chicks, let the mother go: the young you may take for yourself. So shall you prosper and have a long life.'

This prudent use of natural resources is based on ecological wisdom learned over the centuries. It encourages one to eat the produce but to be careful to save the breeding stock, even if this means human privation. In stark contrast, modern agribusiness does not care much about variety in breeding stock. It abandons traditional seed varieties that have been used for hundreds of years and allows them to become extinct, while it narrows the range to a few more lucrative hybrid ones. Transnational corporations such as Royal Dutch Shell and Ciba-Geigy are attempting to control seed production. Since these companies have huge fertilizer and pesticide divisions, there is a danger that only seed requiring high chemical input will be available on the market in the future. By abandoning traditional seed varieties we are in danger of losing the raw material on which many of our food sources depend. Pressure to increase cereal production for animal and human consumption means that farmers are switching to hybrid seeds. In the Philippines, scores of traditional rice varieties are becoming extinct. Many geneticists, echoing the biblical wisdom, warn us that we are courting disaster. As an Irish person I know what the elimination of variety within a particular species can mean. When disease attacks, as it did the potato crop in

Ireland in the 1840s, everything is destroyed and famine, death and desolation follow.

Sin and Redemption

Our discussion of the new story and the biblical teaching on creation underlies that the primary thrust in the whole process is blessing, fruitfulness and life. If this is not clearly appreciated, then everything else is distorted. The Bible, however, is not naive about the reality of evil. Sin, redemption and salvation are important themes in the biblical perspective. But it needs to be emphasized that they do not stand apart and take precedence over creation, as has happened so often in theology and spirituality during recent centuries. Sin, evil, redemption and salvation need to be placed in their proper context, otherwise they are trivialized and not seen in their proper magnitude. If our evil today threatens the whole twenty billion years of creation then it is a very serious business.

The Bible certainly treats it as such. It has a very realistic appreciation of the actuality and power of sin and evil in the world, and of the need to overcome them. But sin in the Bible not only distorts inter-human relations and human–Divine relations, it also affects the life-sustaining harmony between human beings and the Earth. According to Emil Brunner, in *The Christian Doctrine of Creation and Redemption*, estrangement from creatures and from God go hand-in-hand: 'The more man distinguishes himself from the rest of creation, the more he becomes conscious of himself as the subject, as an "I" to whom the world is an object, the more does he tend to confuse himself with God, to confuse his spirit with the spirit of God, and to regard his reason as Divine Reason.'[8]

Just as faithfulness to the Covenant or walking in the way of the Lord brings about order and harmony between people and in the cosmos itself, sin destroys the human friendship with the Divine, induces human misery and brings about cosmic chaos. This was clear in our discussion about the repercussion of the 'original' sin in Genesis. It not only deprived Adam and Eve of God's friendship, but it soured their relationship with the natural world (Gen. 3:17–19). The same holistic concern is evident in Psalm 82:6. The psalmist pleads with God to give judgement on behalf of the weak, the orphans, the destitute and downtrodden because the sins of the wicked shake the very foundations of the Earth.

If sin destroys the harmony between human beings and the natural world, then redemption, to be complete, must heal and renew the primordial unity and recreate the Earth whereever it has been injured through human greed and vice. Unfortunately, this holistic biblical view of redemption has been to the fore neither in the Church's teaching nor, more especially, in its praxis. Many writers feel that a neo-Platonic distrust for the body and natural world held more sway in theological treatises on redemption in recent centuries than the more integrated biblical view. Many neo-Platonists looked on the body as a kind of prison for the soul. Salvation in this view means helping the soul to escape from the confines of the body. Such dualism has no place in Hebrew thought. Salvation involves the total human and Earth reality and thus it has a social, political, economic, ecological as well as an other-worldly dimension.

The theology of redemption in recent years no longer speaks of saving souls but attempts to recapture the all-embracing understanding of the world which is present in the Bible. Redemption is seen as the thorough transformation of individuals in their personal and social lives. As such it embraces the person's social, political and economic activities. Redemption must also bring back balance, harmony and beauty to what has been destroyed in the world. The extent of this is seen in Isaiah 11:5–6 where it even includes healing of the predatory relationships in nature: 'The wolf lives with the lamb, the panther lies down with the kid; calf and lion cub feed together with a little boy to lead them.'

In the New Testament the transformation brought about by the passion, death and resurrection of Christ heals, restores and raises to a new level the intimacy between the human and God. Paul in Ephesians 1:8–12 writes: 'He has made known to us his hidden purpose – such was his will and pleasure determined beforehand in Christ – to be put into effect when the time was ripe: namely, that the universe, all in heaven and on Earth, might be brought into unity in Christ.' (The New English Bible)

The Pauline scholar, Fr Stanislas Lyonnet, commenting on this text, states that Paul wishes to widen as far as possible the redemption brought by Christ. He writes, 'nothing that exists should escape the vital influence of Christ. Each reality, animate, inanimate or personal comes under this influence in a way proper to its own condition, but nothing is deprived of its rebirth.'[9] Once again in Colossians 1:20 Paul sees the reconciliation brought by Christ stretching out to embrace everything in the cosmos: 'Through him God chose to reconcile the whole universe to himself, making peace through the shedding of his blood upon the cross – to reconcile all things, whether on earth or in heaven, through him alone.'

This theme is taken up again in Galatians 3:27–28 where Paul insists that the new community established in Christ breaks down all barriers, cultural, sexist, economic and social. Today, we might add ecological as well. As Paul saw the life, death and resurrection of Jesus extending the boundaries of community to include the above, all that we have seen in the new story and the reality of *Gaia* means that we must extend the barriers further to include everything on this Earth.

The new community established in Christ includes all creation. The most complete and often quoted text which captures this yearning of the created world for the healing touch of God is Romans 8:19–23:

> For the created universe waits with eager expectation for God's sons to be revealed. It was made victim of frustration, not by its own choice, but because of him who made it so; yet always there was hope because the universe itself is to be freed from the shackles of mortality and enter the liberty and splendour of the children of God. Up to the present, we know, the whole created universe groans in all its parts as if in the pangs of childbirth. Not only so, but even we, to whom the Spirit is given as first fruits of the harvest to come, are groaning inwardly while we wait for God to make us his sons and set our whole body free.

Lyonnet in his commentary on this text says that Paul does not wish to 'limit his horizons to the human world alone'.[10] The redemption of the human body and the redemption of the universe are bound together. This and similar texts should give Christians a new stimulus to understand in greater detail the extraordinary mystery of the cosmos; to become aware of the interconnectedness of all beings in this magnificent world. Especially in our times this prophetic Pauline doctrine urges men and women to be conscious that where relationships are fractured there is need for healing of a personal, social and cosmic nature. The creative challenge for soteriology in our time is to reflect on how to link the continuing redemption of human beings, both individually and socially, with the redemption of the Earth.

In the view of many fundamentalists the world is there solely to be used as a resource by human beings. Since this world is doomed to pass away in the very near future, it does not really matter that the natural world is being polluted and plundered to sustain the standard of living of a small segment of humanity. Here again we see that religion, in this case a very inadequate soteriology, can actually act as a stimulus to those who are destroying the natural world. Because of the heightened emphasis on immediate other-world salvation they are blind to the fact that what they are doing is destroying the twenty billion years of God's creation and condemning every succeeding generation to poverty.

7

BRIGHT AND DARK SIDES OF THE CHRISTIAN RESPONSE

Before going on to look at what other religious or cultural traditions might have to offer in our search for a viable theology of creation, it might be useful to look at some approaches to the natural world which are inspired by the biblical perspective and which, in varying degrees, have helped shape Christian consciousness through the centuries. The first two approaches emerge from the Benedictine monastic tradition and the experience of Francis of Assisi. Many people are familiar with these visions of the natural world, because they have left an indelible stamp on western European agricultural and aesthetic traditions. The third strand which I will develop arises from the writings of Hildegarde. Her writings have only become well-known in recent years, so her impact, to date, is still very limited.

Benedictine Care for the Earth

From the seventh century onwards, a network of Benedictine monasteries was established in western Europe. St Benedict of Nursia, the father of western monasticism, decided that his monks should live together in a stable community. The rhythm of the monastic life written into his famous Rule included liturgical and other forms of prayer, manual work and study. This inclusion of manual work was in a sense a revolutionary departure. Greek and Roman scholars in general showed a disdain for manual work. They felt that it was

129

demeaning for the scholar to engage in such a lowly task. By combining work and prayer, Benedict ennobled all kinds of manual work. He also insisted that each monastery should be self-sufficient, so the range of manual work included domestic chores, crafts, garden work, tilling the soil and caring for domestic animals. The stability of the monastery meant that the monks had to learn to cultivate the soil in a renewable way.

They learned to care for the land so that the model of interaction with the natural world to emerge from this tradition might be called the *taming of the Earth*. It was very much an extension of the garden tradition of the Bible itself. The monks set about draining marshes, cutting forests and tilling the soil. Many of the technologies which the monks introduced into the tradition of the European agriculture, far from depleting the soil, actually enhanced its fertility. The monks and the peasants who worked with them exemplify René Dubos' more hopeful thesis elaborated in *Wooing the Earth*, that: 'The interaction between humanity and the Earth often generates more interesting and creative ecosystems than those occuring in the wilderness.[1]

It is easy to understand why this Benedictine ideal of good husbandry and responsible stewardship of land has an appeal for the farmers, like Wendell Berry in the United States, who are campaigning for an end to industrial, high-technology, petroleum-based agriculture which, Berry maintains, is debasing both the soil and the tiller. The Benedictine continuity between a spirituality which receives the land and all its produce as gift, and good husbandry, is captured in this beautiful meditation from the last paragraph of Berry's book, *The Gift of Good Land*.[2]

> To live we must daily break the body and shed the blood of creation. When we do this knowingly, lovingly, skillfully and reverently it is a sacrament. When we do it ignorantly, greedily, clumsily and destructively it is a desecration. In such a desecration we condemn ourselves to spiritual moral loneliness and others to want.

The Benedictine model of relating to the natural world was marked by gratitude for the good things of the Earth and respect for the Earth in order to ensure its continued fruitfulness for human beings. Humans were called to be faithful stewards of the world and not to abuse the Earth. But the point of departure was always the human perspective. There was still a fear that 'raw' nature is unpredictable and capricious and can easily overpower human beings unless constant vigilance is maintained. So the drive to domesticate nature and to bring it under human control was very much at the centre of the Benedictine tradition. Historians also point out that this tradition of caring for land was most effective during the early Benedictine period. Over the years through a variety of means, especially legacies, Benedictine monasteries amassed more land. More and more they became powerful economic and political centres and the superior, the abbot, began to look and act like a feudal lord.

Franciscan Fellowship with all Creation

Unlike Benedict, St Francis of Assisi (1182–1226) was a nomad at heart. He and his friars, who were street preachers, were constantly on the move. They had no possessions and were expected to live lightly on the Earth, a burden neither to the Earth nor to those who met their subsistence needs. In opting for the nomadic life, Francis abandoned any *homo faber* role for the brothers. There is no urge to remake the world, even in the garden tradition of the Benedictines. The natural world is not seen from a utilitarian perspective, as providing food, clothing and shelter for human beings. Rather there is a sense of joy, wonder, praise, and gratitude for the gift of all life. For Francis, every creature in the world was a mirror of God's presence and, if approached correctly, a step leading one to God. What emerges here might be called a *fellowship approach* to creatures. There is no will to dominate or transform nature lurking behind Francis' approach. In his 'Canticle of the Creatures' Francis shows a kinship with, and deep insight into the heart of all creation – animate and inanimate – which is probably unique in the whole European experience.

The Canticle of Brother Sun

Most high, all powerful, all good Lord!
All praise is yours, all glory, all honour and blessing.
To you, alone, Most High, do they belong.
No mortal lips are worthy
To pronounce your name.
All praise be yours, my Lord, through all that you have
made,
And first my Lord Brother Sun,
Who brings the day; and light you give to us through
him.
How beautiful is he, how radiant in all his splendour!
Of you, most high, he bears the likeness.
All praise be yours, my Lord, through Sister Moon and
Stars;
In the heavens you have made them, bright
And precious and fair.
All praise be Yours, my Lord, through Brothers Wind and
Air,
And fair and stormy, all the weather's moods,
By which You cherish all that You have made.
All praise be Yours, my Lord, through the Sister Water,
So useful, lowly, precious and pure.
All praise be Yours, my Lord, through Brother Fire,
Through whom you brighten up the night.
How beautiful he is, how gay! Full of power and
strength.
All praise be yours, my Lord, through Sister Earth, my
mother
Who feeds us in her sovereignty and produces
Various fruits with coloured flowers and herbs.[3]

Francis's language and thought, his 'Brother Sun' and
'Sister Moon', his loving relationship with the wind and water,
resemble more closely the language of India, China or the
North American Chief Seattle tradition than the usual
European, Christian approach to the natural world. Yet he
avoids identifying the Divine exclusively with nature and
denying any transcendent dimension in God. He does this
simply by expanding the Christian call to love God and the

neighbour to include all creation in a way that heals the split between God, the human and nature so characteristic of much of Christian literature before and since.

Francis lived at a period in history of turmoil and change, when a number of what proved to be the most destructive urges in western civilization were just beginning to emerge. He witnessed the move back from an almost exclusively rural economy to market centres. He saw the rise of the mercantile economy which over the next few centuries was to have a profound effect on the way humans related to each other and to the natural world. Francis himself, though born into a fairly wealthy merchant family, did not place any value on money or accumulating wealth, much to the chagrin of his father. In fact, his teaching, and especially his life-style, was a radical critique of money, and of a rising class-consciousness which valued people because of the property they owned. Francis has much to teach us by way of an ecological ethic since our consumer society is obsessed with accumulating wealth to the detriment of the poor and of the Earth itself. Francis felt that reverence for and intimacy with all life precluded any need to own things. A genuine follower of Jesus 'who had no place to lay his head' should only take from the Earth what was necessary for sustaining life.

Francis' love for the natural world has captured the imagination of the West in a unique way. Zeffirelli's film *Brother Sun, Sister Moon* is a modern presentation of Europe's fascination with Francis. While the picture of Francis it portrays lacks an accurate appreciation of Francis' overwhelming passion for God, the fountain from which his love for creatures flowed, it sensitively captures an important facet of his life.

The memory of Francis in our world today is a healing, reconciling and creative one. It inspires many people to become pacifists, to build a true fraternity among humans and to renounce war before it is too late for humanity and the Earth. It also inspires naturalists and ecologists to preserve nature untamed by humans. The protection of wilderness areas in our world today is essential for many reasons. Endangered species need a habitat if they are to survive and not become extinct. Experiencing the wilderness is an expanding and uplifting sensation for the human spirit. It draws us out beyond our own selves. An untamed environment, untouched by human beings, whether it is a vast ocean, a rain forest or a desert, points to the ultimate mystery at the heart of the world which continually calls human beings to a deeper communion with the Earth and with God. Francis, the saint for all seasons, is particularly important today and so is a happy choice as the patron of ecologists.

Hildegarde of Bingen: The Greening of the Earth

The approach of Hildegarde of Bingen (1098–1178) adds a unique dimension to both that of Benedict and Francis. Unfortunately, her writings are not widely known. Selections from her writings have only been published in English in the last few years. This remarkable woman – poet, musician, painter, visionary, botanist, herbalist, counsellor to the popes, princes and councils of the Church – has a unique contribution to make to the western Christian's appreciation of the natural world. Her approach to the Earth delights in the 'greening of the Earth'.

The Divine is present in the 'greening' of the Earth in a way reminiscent of the fertility poetry of the pre-Christian Celtic religion of much of Europe. Hildegarde captures and celebrates in her writings the uniquely feminine experience of the most intimate processes of the natural world. The taming, organizing skills of Benedict and even the fraternal solicitude for all creatures of Francis are valuable elements of a masculine approach to reality. But Hildegarde celebrates the feminine, fertility dimension. Her poetry pulsates with a rapturous, sensuous love for the Earth. It is full of ardour and passion. In the following poem she delights in the love of the Creator for the creation and does not feel constrained to shy away from explicitly sexual language. 'I compare the great love of Creator and creation to the same love and fidelity with which God binds man and woman together. This is so that together they might be creatively fruitful.'[4]

There is no ambiguity towards creation in Hildegarde; no revulsion at the mention of earthly, bodily or inanimate nature. She does not see the world as evil or corrupting, to be subdued and tamed through ascetical practices. Unlike the writings of many Christian mystics before and since, the person seeking sanctity is not encouraged to run away from the natural world. Hildegarde insists that 'holy persons draw to themselves all that is earthly'. For her, the natural world is not an area of chaos or wilderness which humans must either avoid or do battle with in order to conquer and domesticate. Nature evokes joy, wonder, praise, awe and especially love. She is so beautifully adorned that even her creator approaches her in the guise of a lover to embrace her with a kiss.

> As the Creator loves his creation
> so creation loves the Creator.
> Creation, of course, was fashioned to be adorned
> to be showered
> to be gifted with the love of the Creator
> The entire world has been embraced by this kiss.[5]

Many cultures around the world revere the Earth as mother and celebrate her fruitfulness. It is not surprising then that Hildegarde takes up this image. The nourishing role of the Earth is not confined to our biological needs but includes our emotional and spiritual well-being. Finally, the Earth is most creative in moulding the very flesh of the Son of God.

> The Earth is at the same time mother
> She is mother of all
> For contained in her
> are the seeds of all
> The Earth of humankind
> contains all moistness
>   all verdancy
>   all germinating power
> It is in so many ways fruitful
> Yet it forms not only the basic
> raw material for humankind
> but also the substance of God's Son.[6]

Hopefully, when her writings are better known, Hildegarde will assume her rightful place in Christian spirituality. In her company we may be able to overcome the deep-seated fear and hostility for the natural world which is found so frequently in Christian spiritual guides, ancient and modern. With her we can leave aside the gloom, pessimism and guilt that commonly haunt Christian spirituality and joyfully recognize God's presence in the world around us.

In the modern world, women are often to the fore in both the peace movement and the ecological movement. They can more easily identify with the pain and destruction which the Earth is experiencing at the hands of a male-dominated world since they have also been victims. One thinks, for example, of the women camped for a number of years at Greenham Common in England, protesting against the installation of Cruise and Pershing II missiles in western Europe. It is a pity the creation-affirming writings of Hildegarde are not more readily available to them as they protest on behalf of all peoples and the Earth herself at the stupidity of pretending that anyone's security rests in weapons which, if ever used, will bring death to everything on Earth.

Christian Responsibility

Above I have presented the bright side of Christians' caring for the Earth. But as I have mentioned there is also a dark side in our tradition. A theology of creation must also criticize our traditional presentation of important themes of our faith so that, neither in their religious form nor in subsequent secular manifestations, do they, wittingly or unwittingly, contribute to the destruction of the Earth. In this connection it is worth calling attention to a controversy which has engaged ecologists, theologians and historians of technology in recent years regarding the specifically Christian responsibility for the ecological crisis. The controversy centres around the question why modern science and technology emerged from a Christian culture and not from a Chinese or Indian or even the Islamic world.

Lynn White, an American historian, addressed this question in a now famous lecture delivered at the American Association for the Advancement of Science, in 1966.[7] In his lecture he indicts the Christian tradition and maintains that our present ecological troubles will continue until there is a major shift in westerners' religious perspective. White maintains that westerners feel 'superior to nature, contemptuous of it, and willing to use it for our slightest whim'. He continues:

> We shall continue to have a worsening ecological crisis until we reject the Christian axiom that nature has no reason for existence but to serve man... Both our present science and technology are so tinctured with orthodox Christian arrogance towards nature that no solution for our ecological crisis can be expected from them alone. Since the roots of our troubles are so largely religious, the remedy also must be essentially religious, whether we call it so or not.

René Dubos, the renowned ecologist and microbiologist, disputes White's charge in *Wooing The Earth*,[8] pointing out that extensive environmental degradation began long before the biblical era. He maintains that almost every civilization – Chinese, Greek, Roman, Aztec and even Hindu Indian and Buddhist Southeast Asia – abused their environment to some degree by deforestation and over-intensive grazing. He recalls how Plato in the *Critias* compared the land of Attica 'to the bones of a wasted body'.

Others feel that national and cultural factors may have been the primary determinants in spurring the development of technology in the West since eastern Christianity produced a mystical civilization indifferent to earthly progress. While this might be true, it seems more reasonable to assume that a confluence of influences, cultural and religious, set the stage for the rapid development of science in Europe from the sixteenth century onwards.

In the sixteenth century, for example, Chinese science was much more advanced than western science. The Chinese had discovered printing, the principle of magnetism, explosives, advanced technologies for metal casting and a vast array of medical and astronomical knowledge; yet their scientific thrust stagnated while western science advanced. Some commentators attribute the advance in empirical science in western Europe to a notion which is central to the Newtonian view of the world – that the laws governing the physical universe are independent of the realities themselves. Fundamentally, this is a religious idea. The roots of this conception can be traced back to the Bible where Yahweh is seen as the supreme lawgiver who places all the realities in the universe in their proper place. The order, structure and intelligibility of nature means that the laws of nature can be known through observation and experiment and then used to transform nature herself.

That science and technology arose, at least in part, from the religious well-springs of the European experience seems to me very difficult to deny. I feel that much of the weight of history is on the side of a modified version of White's thesis. But White overstates his case. For a historian baldly to label something as "Christian orthodoxy," without qualification, shows little understanding of the rich and varying strands that co-exist together and often supplant each other in the Bible and down through the centuries since then. We have seen that, while the Bible does insist on separating both the Divine and the human from the natural world, other strands within the tradition emphasize the need to respect the Earth. In the brief look at Christian ecological models discussed above, Benedict who cared for the earth, Francis who saw creatures as all part of the extended family, and Hildegarde who delighted in the Earth are surely as Christian as James Watt – a recent United States Secretary of the Interior – who attempted to justify his anti-ecological land programme by appealing to the biblical command to 'occupy the land'.

It would have to be admitted that they may not always have had as powerful an impact as one might have wished. My own thesis in this book is that the overemphasis on redemption, particularly when human destiny is divorced from that of the natural world, has prepared the ground for a technology which is increasingly causing the deterioration of the Earth community. As Christians we must be very watchful lest the mythic aura which surrounds any of our religious ideas about the world contributes in any way to the destruction of the Earth.

The Notion of Progress

One such idea is the notion of progress and development. This is one of the most important and constantly discussed issues today. In many ways it is probably the most dynamic notion in modern history. It finds a central place in both capitalism and Marxism. So what is implied by the term and how does one gauge it? It seems impossible to define it without seeing it within the context of both technology and western Christianity. In popular perception today, the less dependent people are on the natural world and the more they are surrounded by technology, the more progress they consider they are making. This understanding is so pervasive that even today, when the human community is involved in extensive devolution, irreversibly affecting the Earth community on a scale of hundreds of millions of years, we are still so dazzled by new machines that we continue to call what is happening "progress."

The notion of progress is also tied up with our religious tradition. At the end of his book, *The History of the Idea of Progress*, Robert Nisbet, having completed a survey of the idea over two thousand years, asks the question, What is the future of the idea of the progress? Immediately he asks a more basic question:

> What is the future of Judeo-Christianity in the West? For if there is one generalization that can be made confidently about the history of the idea it is that throughout its history the idea has been closely linked with, has depended upon, religion or upon intellectual constructs derived from religion.[9]

In the West it appears that the idea of continual progress is the dynamism behind the technological drive to transform the Earth. As Nisbet sees it, this powerhouse is itself dependent on a religious understanding of reality. In fact it is visionary. It presents human beings with a secularized and debased version of the millenial age spoken of in the Book of Daniel in the Old Testament and the Book of Revelation in the New Testament. These speak of a time when an angel will seize the dragon and chain him for a thousand years (Rev. 20:2). The reign of the saints will begin, an era of peace and justice will prevail and the Kingdom will be established on Earth. Thus the pain and difficulty of the human condition will be finally overcome.

This belief in inevitable progress fuelled by a millenial drive has a long history in western consciousness. It was particularly powerful during the medieval period. In the twelfth century, for example, Joachim de Fiore used this millenial approach to divide all history into three progressive epochs. The first age was dominated by the Father and corresponds to the Old Testament. The New Testament period is the age of the Son, and the age that is about to be born, the end times, will be the age of the Spirit. The idea of a progressive unfolding also runs through the historical writings of Giambattista Vico (1668–1744). He moved the idea from the spiritual realm to the plane of secular history.

While Vico retained a place for God in his schema, Auguste Comte (1798–1857), Karl Marx (1818–83) and others dethroned the Divine. According to these and other writers of the time, human beings were on their own and could not look for salvation elsewhere. Since it seemed that an extensive change in the human condition, particularly the drive to overcome the difficulties and pain of this world, was not going to come from God, then human beings themselves must set about creating a new, more tolerable world, mainly through the use of technology.

A future-oriented, progressively improving world achieved mainly through technology is central to both Marxism and capitalism in today's world. In both of these ideological systems the attention of people is riveted on a condition of future bliss. The present is expendable for the sake of future glory. People are asked to put up with squalor and tyranny today in order that the future may be bright and rosy for their children. In the Marxist scheme the bright future is infallibly guaranteed by the dynamics of history – which for both Marx and Lenin includes extensive industrialization – and the revolutionary process. In capitalism the era of abundance and future bliss is ensured by private enterprise, the workings of the free market and technology. Once again ordinary people are encouraged to be patient and even to condone the excesses of the sweat shops. The proponents of this view ask for a few more decades of sacrifice before there is plenty for everyone.

Religious people would do well to remember that the mystic appeal surrounding the notion of progress on which the two illusory worlds above are based is firmly linked to the religious idea of 'the glory to come'. It is co-opted and, of course, debased by these two economic systems whose impact on the real world is exploitative and destructive.

Nowhere is this more evident than in the realm of advertising. This is one of the most important growth areas for modern industrial societies. In Britain alone $5925 million dollars was spent on advertising in 1981. The advertiser sets out to induce mass purchase of his or her product. Joy, beauty, health, sexual appeal or whatever constitutes a wonderworld is confidently promised to the user of the latest product or gadget. The advertisement do not call attention to the fact that the deodorant spray may well deplete the ozone region or that the hot dog and fast foods are destroying the tropical forests. They may be forced to tell the public that cigarette smoking is dangerous to a person's health, but it is done in such a way that the warning is hardly seen. Finally, the advertising message beamed at the public conveniently forgets that planned obsolescence is an important element in modern industrial societies. Within the space of a few short years the gadgets which today have a glittering appeal will end up on the junk heap.

Given the destruction which much of our industrial processes are bringing to the Earth in both Marxist and capitalist countries, one might ask, 'What good is a classless society in a barren and poisoned land?' No matter how equitable the social system might be in the future, if the land loses its topsoil, it will cease to produce food for every creature, including human beings. The capitalist dream of plenty for those with drive and initiative, eventually trickling down to nourish the less fortunate, will never be realized, for the simple reason that there will be nothing left to trickle down. Grinding poverty and squalor will be the lot of the vast majority of human beings with little hope that their descendants will fare any better.

This discussion should awaken us to the fact that we must look carefully at our language to discover the real meaning of the words we use. Much of what we commonly call progress today – digging up the Earth, poisoning it and destroying natural diversity – is retardation for the Earth community. We need to call things by their proper names in order to reverse the destruction which has already taken place so extensively. Real progress will also involve healing this damage.

Christians must be particularly sensitive to the fact that secularized versions of our millenial and redemption myths do indeed underlie destructive drives which are causing worldwide ecological deterioration. The best way to ensure that no formulation of our Christian faith ever lends its weight to ideologies that in practice turn much of the world into junk is to resituate our faith, especially our understanding of redemption, within a holistic theology of the emergent creation.

8

DIALOGUE WITH OTHER RELIGIONS

In the previous three chapters we saw that a contemporary theology of creation must be grounded in an adequate cosmology and the rich themes in the biblical revelation and Christian tradition. Our theology can be enriched even further with the wisdom and rich insights from a number of the great religions and, especially, from creative dialogue with traditional (primal) religions. In our account of the emergence of human beings we saw that, while the great civilizations elaborated their understanding of the world in relative isolation from each other, today they are constantly impinging on and enriching one another.

One very fruitful outcome of the 'collectivization of humanity', to use the phrase of Teilhard, is that today all humanity is heir to the total human venture. In the past twenty-five years, for example, Christian meditation has been profoundly affected by oriental prayer forms, particularly from Buddhism and Hinduism. Christian prayer can never again be adequately studied without reference to these creative developments. In other ways also the creative dialogue between religions which we see taking place all around us is enriching each religion in its own self-understanding, and thereby the collective religious experience of humanity is enhanced.

The following are a few brief examples of what Asian religions have to teach us about the Earth. B. Radhakrishna

Rao, writing on ecology in Vedic literature in the magazine called *Mazingira*,[1] points out that the Vedas contain many appeals to human beings to treat animals kindly and to experience the divine presence in the hills, mountains, valleys, rivers, and forests of the Indian sub-continent. The *Rig-Veda*, for example, encourages the listener to form friendships with animals and even with inanimate objects:

Strong one, make me strong,
May all the beings look on me with the eye of a friend,
May I look on all beings with the eye of a friend,
May we look on one another with the eye of a friend.

In the *Upanishads* there is a clear understanding of the fact that things in nature are interrelated. The following stanza from *Isvyasopanishad* shows a keen awareness of the delicate balance of nature and how easy it is to interrupt the cycle of nature:

For food to grow, rains have been made a part of the universe; the system can work only if the living creatures can accept the system consisting of the different facets which are interdependent.[2]

Human beings are encouraged to be compassionate and to practise self-restraint. The following invocation prays for peace everywhere.

The peace in the sky, the peace in the mid-air,
The peace on the Earth, the peace in water,
The peace in plants, the peace in forest trees,
The peace in all the Devas, the peace in ultimate reality.
The peace in all things,
The peace in peace,
May that peace come to us.[3]

This respect and compassion for life is also found in the second great religion to emerge in the Indian sub-continent – Buddhism. Its precepts enjoin all the faithful to seek a right livelihood. An essential dimension of right livelihood is concern for the life of all creatures. The demands on the monk are even more strict. He is forbidden to take any life. These are two elements of the overarching Buddhist virtue of compassion for all reality. This compassion and respect for all creatures, irrespective of their utilitarian value or close relationship with the individual, is beautifully expressed in a poem quoted in Thomas Berry's book, *Buddhism.*[4]

May every creature abound
in well-being and in peace.

May every living being, weak or strong
The long and the small
The short and the medium-sized
the mean and the great.

May every living being, seen and unseen
Those dwelling far-off, those near-by
Those already born, those waiting to be born
May all attain inward peace.

Let no one deceive another
Let no one despise another in any situation
Let no one from antipathy or hatred
Wish evil to anyone at all.

Just as a mother with her own life
Protects her son, her only son, from hurt,
So within your own self foster
A limitless concern for every living creature.

Display a heart of boundless love
For all the world
In all its height and depth and broad extent
Love unrestrained, without hate or enmity
Then as you stand or walk, sit or lie,
Until overcome by drowsiness
Devote your mind entirely to this.
It is known as living here a life divine.

In September 1985 I spent two weeks in China with a group of social scientists, many of whom are involved in dialogue between religions in Asia. During our tour we met representatives of the Protestant and Catholic Churches in China and of the Muslim and Buddhist Associations of China in a number of cities. All spoke about the resurgence of religion in China and what it meant for their people. I was interested to note that only the Buddhists, in the person of Mr Zhao Puchu, spoke about the environment and the preservation of species. Buddhists have much to share with other religious traditions in this area.

This concern for all creatures is also evident in Chinese literature. The neo-Confucian literature particularly abhorred any dualism that would separate the Earth from the heavens, the soul from the body, or the human from the natural world. According to Wang Yang-ming (1472–1529), the hallmark of the great person is to avoid any such dualism, to seek unity in all things and to have an abiding love for all creation. Only in this way could a person reach full stature. Altruistic behaviour is seen to benefit all members of the body of nature, including the individual human person. Self-centred action harms the body of nature and leads to disaster for every creature:

> The great Person considers Heaven and Earth and all beings as one Body. He/She considers the world as one family and the nation as one Person. Those who make artificial divisions between themselves and others are persons of spiritual immaturity... everything from ruler, administrator, husband, wife, and friends, to mountains, rivers, spirits, birds, animals, and plants must be deeply loved in order to comprehend and actualize my own humanity that constitutes One Body with them. Only then will I truly be One Body with Heaven, Earth and all the things.[5]

Another neo-Confucian text commonly known as the 'Western Inscription'[6] shares this intimate personal relationship with all reality. The author does not insist on an imperial, superior position for the human. Human beings find their true place within the natural scheme of things. In this way humans are co-extensive with the universe in a way that comes quite close to the Teilhardian view. Westerners have much to learn from this comprehensive identification with the natural world which is foreign to the greater part of our own humanist tradition. Keith Thomas, in his recent book *Man and the Natural World*, draws attention to the fact that even at the beginning of the sixteenth century western literature and theological tradition ascribed no intrinsic meaning to the natural world or accorded to it any rights apart from its role in serving human kind.[7]

Most westerners even today would be uneasy with the thought expressed in the following quotation. Yet it is a refreshing antidote to the dualistic traditions of western thought:

> Heaven is my father and Earth is my mother, and even such a small creature as I find an intimate place in their midst. Therefore that which extends throughout the universe I regard as my body and that which directs the universe I consider my nature. All people are my brothers and sisters, and all things are my companions.[8]

Tribal Religious Experience

There is also a wealth of helpful insights from the diverse and wide-ranging traditional (primal) religious tradition which I referred to in the tribal phase of the evolution of culture. In Chapter 5 and also here I am using an epochal approach to tribal societies and civilizations as I believe it is both valid and helpful for the purposes of this study. However, as one living in the province of South Cotabato where there are seven distinct tribal cultures – if one includes the dubious claims that the famous Tasaday are in fact a separate group – I am well aware of the tendency of many writers to lump together these quite disparate societies under the label tribal societies. While not glossing over the marked differences that distinguish tribal societies, it is both accurate and helpful to point to dominant themes in many tribal societies though they might be articulated in different ways in each individual culture.

In contrast to the biblical tradition which, as we saw, identifies the divine/human encounter primarily in historical events, primal religions endow the natural world with psychic powers. The believers here relate to the natural world as a *Thou*. Sometimes the emphasis is on reverence and wonder, at other times the natural world is feared, so that the believer must placate the spirits with ritual offerings. At all times, however, the world is alive with spirit presence. Nature is not inert, secularized or a mere *It*, to be used as a resource for the exclusive benefit of humans. Nature has its own inner presence and dignity apart from any value humans may place upon it. As such it must be revered and respected.

This sacred, non-utilitarian view of nature is captured very strikingly in a letter which Chief Seattle of the Duwamish tribe from Washington State wrote to the American President in 1854 in response to a request by the government to buy the Indian lands and relocate the tribe on a reservation. The chief's letter does not dwell on the economic value of the land or haggle over what is considered a fair price. Even the future of his tribe in the reservation does not unduly concern the chief – it is only mentioned once. Because he is a keen observer of the white man's destructive ways, the chief is very concerned about what will happen to the land, the rivers, the mountains, the air and the beasts of the land under the onslaught of white settlers, who are fanning across the land and in the Indians' view destroying it.

Chief Seattle's letter displays an intimacy with, and understanding of, the natural world which is almost completely outside the realm of experience for western people, because for so long our tradition has insisted on placing the human outside the natural world. Chief Seattle finds the white man's approach to nature lacking in warmth, tenderness and compassion. It is proud, arrogant, contemptuous, and ultimately suicidal. The text written over one hundred years ago has a prophetic ring about it; his critique of western man's behaviour is tragically even more relevant and accurate today. I will quote at length from this great man's letter as it might help spark within us a similar sense of compassion for all things and a realization that everything is interconnected. Ultimately we tamper with it at our own peril.

The Earth is Sacred

How can you buy or sell the sky, the warmth of the land? The idea is strange to us. If we do not own the freshness of the air and the sparkle of the water, how can you buy them?

Every part of this earth is sacred to my people. Every shining pine needle, every sandy shore, every mist in the dark woods, every clearing and humming insect is holy in the memory and experience of my people. The sap which courses through the trees carries the memories of the red man. The white man's dead forget the country of their birth when they go to walk among the stars. Our dead never forget this beautiful earth, for it is the mother of the red man. We are part of the earth and it is part of us. The perfumed flowers are our sisters; the deer, the horse, the great eagle, these are our brothers. The rocky crests, the juices in the meadows, the body heat of the pony, and man – all belong to the same family.

So, when the Great Chief in Washington sends word that he wishes to buy our land, he asks much of us. The Great Chief sends word he will reserve us a place so that we can live comfortably among our own people. He will be our Father and we will be his children. So we will consider your offer to buy our land. But it will not be easy. For this land is sacred to us.

The shining water that moves in the streams and rivers is not just water but the blood of our ancestors. If we sell you the land, you must remember that it is sacred, and you must teach your children that each ghostly reflection in the clear water of the lakes tells of events and memories in the life of my people. The water's murmur is the voice of the father's father.

Kindness to the Rivers

The rivers are our brothers, they quench our thirst. The rivers carry our canoes, and feed our children. If we sell you our land, you must remember, and teach your children, that the rivers are our brothers, and yours, and you must henceforth give the rivers the kindness you would give a brother.

We know that the white man does not understand our ways. One portion of land is the same to him as the next,

for he is a stranger who comes in the night and takes from
the land whatever he needs. The Earth is not his brother,
but his enemy, when he has conquered it, he moves on.
He leaves his father's graves behind, and he does not
care. He kidnaps the earth from his children, and he does
not care. His father's graves, and his children's
birthright, are forgotten. He treats his mother, the earth,
and his brother, the sky, as things to be bought,
plundered, sold like sheep or bright beads. His appetite
will devour the earth and leave behind only a desert.

I do not know. Our ways are different from yours. The
sight of your cities pains the eyes of the red man. But
perhaps it is because the red man is a savage and does not
understand. There is no quiet place in the white man's
cities; no place to hear the unfurling of leaves in spring,
or the rustle of the insect's wings. The clatter only seems
to insult the ears. And what is there to life if a man
cannot hear the lonely cry of the whippoorwill, or the
argument of the frogs around a pond at night? The
Indian prefers the soft sound of the wind darting over the
face of a pond, and the smell of wind itself, cleansed by
the midday rain, or scented with the pinon pine.

The Air is Precious

The air is precious to the red man, for all things share the
same breath – the beast, the tree, and the human. The
white man does not seem to notice the air he breathes.
Like a man dying for many days he is numb to the
stench. But if we sell you our land you must remember
that the air is precious to us, that the air shares its spirit
with all the life it supports. The wind that gave our
grandfather his first breath also receives his last sigh.
And if we sell you our land, you must keep it apart and
sacred, as a place where even the white man can go to
taste the wind that is sweetened by the meadow's flowers.

All Things are Connected

So we will consider your offer to buy our land. If we
decide to accept, I will make one condition; the white

man must treat the beasts of this land as his brothers. I
have seen a thousand rotting buffaloes on the prairie, left
by the white man who shot them from a passing train. I
am a savage and I do not understand how the smoking
iron horse can be more important that the buffalo that we
kill only to stay alive. What is man without the beasts? If
all the beasts were gone, man would die from great
loneliness of spirit, for whatever happens to the beast also
happens to man. All things are connected. Whatever
befalls the earth befalls the sons of earth. The white man,
too, shall pass – perhaps sooner than other tribes.
Continue to contaminate your bed, and you will one
night suffocate in your own waste. When the buffalo are
all slaughtered, the wild horses all tamed, the secret
corners of the forest heavy with scent of many men, and
the view of ripe hills blotted by talking wires, where is
the thicket? Gone. Where is the eagle? Gone. And what is
it to say goodbye to the swift pony and the hunt? It is the
end of living and the beginning of survival.[9]

There are many other examples from the North American
Indian tradition to show that they considered all of nature as
interrelated and functioning as a whole. The human is part of
the whole and should be disturbed when other creatures are
not respected. Vine Deloria, in *God is Red*, recalls that a
Cayuse Indian called Young Chief refused to sign the Treaty
of Walla Walla because the wider creation was not properly
represented and protected.[10]

Many other tribal people have a similar feeling for, and
intimacy with, the Earth. In the creation story among the
T'boli, describing the origins of their most important lake –
Lake Sebu – the first words uttered by the first human being
called *Kludan* are, 'what a privilege it is to be called upon to
care for the Earth and the Sky'. The story goes on to describe
the interdependence of the community of the living. A small
bird called the *betoti* and one of the ants were responsible for
discovering soil and making it fruitful so that all creatures,
including humans, would have a secure and fruitful place to
live.

The above examples are merely pointers to how fruitful the
dialogue between different religious and humanist traditions

can be in developing a wide-ranging and relevant theology of creation for our times, when the Earth is crying out for recognition, respect, and care. The Christian understanding of history and of God's action in history, particularly in the person of Jesus, has much to contribute to other religions and cultures, particularly in the priority which is given to the personal dimension of human existence. This has helped to establish the parameters of personal freedom in many societies where Christianity has taken root. This respect for freedom has given an enormous boost to human creativity in many cultures.

Yet it must be recognized that the Christian vision is also partial and like every other tradition is vulnerable and needs to engage in dialogue with other traditions. We have seen above that Christians have much to gain from the intimacy with nature which other religions have developed over the centuries. The Japanese poet, Ninomiya Sontoku (1787–1856), finds the path of sincerity primarily in the book of the cosmos. For him it has priority over other sacred books:

> The path of truth is laid out before us in the scriptures of the cosmos. Many scholars confine their study of the true way to books but I find the fullness of truth written in the heavens and the earth. Human beings should open their eyes and read this book of the cosmos in order to seek the truth therein.[11]

Cosmic and Earth revelation is, after all, the primary revelation of God. It is also the common heritage of all human beings and so can provide a fruitful basis for dialogue between religious people. A new spirituality which sees the Earth as permeated with the divine presence would undoubtedly provide the basis for world-wide co-operation among religious people today to respect and care for the Earth. I believe that this new religious sense, especially among Christians, must permeate our concern for the Earth.

In the past and even today the Judeo-Christian tradition has displayed a remarkable ability to incorporate rich traditions from outside. Two of the greatest theologians of the Christian era, St Augustine and St Thomas Aquinas, elaborated the Christian faith within the framework of Platonic and

Aristotelian philosophy in order to make it more relevant to their times. Today in Latin America, liberation theologians are doing the same with Marxism. Confronted with the growing ecological challenge we are challenged to open our minds and hearts to the wisdom of the scientific tradition and the creative vision of other religions in our efforts to respond adequately to the central problem of our times. If Christians succeed in bringing about this transformation, a healthy, bountiful future will be in store for the Earth and human beings. We will be able to sing joyfully *The Canticle of the Three Young Men*:

'Bless the Lord, all you works of the Lord,
praise and exalt him above all forever.' (Dan. 3:57)

9

LITURGIES OF EARTH AND FIRE

Thus far this book has attempted to describe some of the most pressing ecological problems facing both the planet and particular bio-regions on Earth like the Philippines and Ireland. It then traced some broad historical movements which are in one way or another responsible for getting us into the present mess, and for continuing to cloud the seriousness of the problem facing the whole Earth community. Chapter 5, inspired by Teilhard's vision of the emergent cosmos, provides a sure foothold for a new sensitivity to the Earth and a new way of living for human beings. Part 2, Chapters 6–8, explores the depths of the Catholic and other religious traditions in order to awaken among Christian people a new respect for the Earth. All of this adds up to the need for a profound revolution which must touch and transform every aspect of modern life – our political, economic, educational, religious and communication institutions.

In my brief sketch of the world-wide ecological situation in Chapter 2, I pointed out that many people are concerned about what is happening and are working to bring about this revolution. Organizations like the Friends of the Earth are trying to raise public awareness of ecological issues at a local and international level. Appropriate technologies to meet local needs in farming and craft skills are being developed. Much of the change in this area derives from the inspiration of E.F. Schumacher's *Small is Beautiful*[1] and the institute – Intermediate Technology Development Group Ltd – which he founded in London. The political ramifications of this new movement are evident today, especially in Europe, in the rapid rise of the Green Party in Germany. Fritjof Capra's and

Charlene Spretnak's *Green Politics: Global Promise*[2] tells this story and assesses the future impact of Green politics on other countries, especially the United States.

This revolution will not take off or be sustained unless the new story becomes the basis of universal education. Christian Churches, with their vast network of schools in almost every country on Earth, could play a very significant role here. This is particularly necessary at the moment when politicians, mesmerized by what they see as the high profits to be gleaned from high technology industries, are goading educational institutions to become even more specialized.[3] Here the work of Ivan Illich[4] and Paulo Freire[5] raises serious questions regarding some of the presuppositions on which our formal schooling is based. At the moment schools, colleges and universities as institutions do not seem to have any real grasp of the magnitude of the problem facing the planet, despite the admirable work being done by individuals here and there. How an educational institute might go about restructuring its curriculum to take on this broader perspective and equip the students to be really creative in the age of *Gaia* is the subject of an essay by Fr Thomas Berry.[6] Some of these ideas are already being put into practice in Elizabeth Seton College in New York.

Much has also been written on how this new understanding would change the face of medicine, away from an over-concentration on curative medicine, back to a more holistic understanding of health care. Even the supposedly practical science of economics has not been left untouched. Many people argue that local communities should move away from an exclusive dependence on a money economy. This would involve people growing their own food and returning to the age-old tradition of barter. As far as I know, little has been written about how this revolution might affect the worship and practice of the Church. The remaining part of this book will be devoted to pointing out briefly how liturgy, sacramental practice, moral response, spirituality and finally mission outreach might be enriched and transformed by this new vision.

Liturgy is one of the most powerful and fruitful areas in which to begin our search to integrate a new vision of the cosmos into our religious life. Since the emergence of human

beings on Earth, women and men have sought to express the
deepest mysteries of their own life and the rhythms of the
Earth and cosmos through myths, rituals and ceremonies.
This is very evident in the celebrations of tribal religions and
particularly the two great Asian religions, Hinduism and
Buddhism.

Even the Christian faith and the Catholic liturgical cycle,
though primarily concerned with celebrating the historical
events like the Exodus and especially the memory of the
passion, death and resurrection of Jesus, is not completely
divorced from the natural world. Each day at morning and
evening, the *Prayer of the Church* reminds us that sunrise and
sunset are sacred moments. The liturgical calendar is linked to
the cycle of the seasons, at least, in the northern hemisphere.
Even the date of Easter, the most important feast celebrating
the paschal mystery of Jesus, is fixed by the cycles of the
moon. Daily, monthly and yearly the Church invites people to
pause and to enter into these sacred moments in order to give
thanks and praise to God for his goodness to us. The
sacraments, too, all draw upon elements of the natural world.
We use bread, water, fire, oil, light and darkness in our
celebrations.

Nevertheless it appears that the polarities set up by the
neo-Platonic dualism I discussed on page 126 which separates
body and soul, heaven and Earth, has had such a powerful
effect on the Christian experience that it has weakened, and
even cut off, those roots in the natural world which should
have been so natural for a highly sacramental religion.
Consider the Eucharist, for example. This celebration makes
present the memory of Jesus in the breaking of bread and the
sharing of the óne cup. The symbols are food and drink which
are shared in the memory of Jesus. Any priest, religious or
teacher who has ever prepared a child for First Communion
knows that the shiny, plastic-like, white, wafer-thin hosts
neither look, smell nor taste like bread. Until recently, the cup
was not shared with lay-people and even now is only given on
'special' occasions. Thus there is scarcely any experience of
the symbolism of drinking. Yet we know that if the flow
between the symbol and the reality that it symbolizes is
severed, the ability of the worshippers to enter deeply into the
reality expressed and celebrated in the symbol is diminished.

The writings of men and women like Paul Tillich, Paul Ricoeur, Mary Douglas, Clifford Geertz and Victor Turner[7] have, during the past two decades, increased our understanding of the power of symbols to transform our personal and social lives. Symbols are most transforming when they are cast in the appropriate cultural idiom of a people and touch their deepest aspirations. They are weakest and least effective when the symbolic meaning has to be explained. In the case of the Eucharist, the child has first to be told that the substance used is bread. The situation is even worse in a country where bread is not the staple food. In the Philippines, for example, where wheat is not grown and has to be imported at the cost of somewhere close to $100 million dollars each year, bread is a luxury food of the middle and upper classes. So when the Eucharist is celebrated in the Philippines, the inner dynamic of the food symbol is foreign, since the staple food of most Filipinos is rice. Poor people are asked to give thanks to God for the memory of Jesus by sharing food and drink that is foreign to their culture. No genuinely inculturated religion can take root in such foreign soil.

A genuine revolution is called for in the use of natural symbols in our liturgies if we hope to capture the religious imagination of people and transform their lives. Food and drink must be real, substantial food and drink so that the symbolic meaning flows directly from the experience of the symbols. This is necessary because the transforming power of a celebration like the Eucharist comes from associating the memory of the life, death and resurrection of Jesus, and all that this entails in terms of a vision of a Christian community, with the very satisfying experience of sharing food and drink. Once the connection is broken the symbol is truncated and ineffectual. Maimed symbols are alienating rather than transforming. They are the last thing we need to celebrate the story of the cosmos and crucial events in that story like the passion, death and resurrection of Jesus.

With some notable exceptions, there is also a lack of feeling for the Earth in many of the prayers of the Catholic liturgy. The final prayer in the Mass of the Second Sunday of Advent in the new liturgy invites the worshippers to 'love the things of heaven and judge wisely the things of Earth'. While it is an improvement on '*doceas nos terrena despicere et amare caelestia* (to despise the things of Earth and love the things of Heaven)', it is surely out of place in the liturgy today. Many liturgical prayers are, at best, indifferent towards the natural world, and this at a time when we are poisoning lakes, acid rain is corroding the beautiful stained glass windows in many of the medieval cathedrals and destroying the walls of churches, and huge engineering projects are tearing the Earth apart. By addressing God, in the second preface of Lent, 'you teach us to live in this passing world with our hearts set on the world that will never end', the Church is unwittingly legitimizing the behaviour of those who destroy the Earth. If the real world is somewhere else and this world ephemeral and unimportant, then it hardly matters how we treat the latter.

Instead of encouraging an attitude of indifference which is destructive, the liturgies of every religion today should inculcate an attitude of compassion, respect and love for the Earth. The opening prayer for the seventeenth Sunday in Ordinary Time is a good example of a prayer that is sensitive to God's presence in the beauty of creation: 'God, our Father, open our eyes to see your hand at work in the splendour of creation and in the beauty of human life. Touched by your hands our world is holy. Help us to cherish the gifts that surround us... and to experience the joy of life in your presence.'

Each celebration should encourage men and women to become more aware of the fruitfulness, beauty, abundance and yet extraordinary fragility of the Earth. Liturgies that use the symbols of the sun, the Earth, water, food, light, darkness, moon and sky should celebrate the story of the cosmos and call attention to the cosmic damage now taking place.

One way to do this would be to institute a Feast of Creation. Our liturgies in some way celebrate the renewing cycle of nature, of seasonal change or the recurring cycle of the Earth, the moon and the sun. However, we have no ritual celebration for the original moments of the emergent cosmos. We should celebrate that most sacred moment – the initial fireball. Without that mystery of energy and fire, nothing in time or space would ever have existed. The formation of the stars, the birth of our sun and planet Earth present unique opportunity for ritual. A ritual focused on nurturing could celebrate the gradual emergence of the ocean as both the mother and cradle of life. Water has such a central role in the liturgies of almost every religion and culture including our own. Each new moment in the progressive unfolding of life – the appearance of plants, flowers, animals, birds and humans – presents its own special possibility for creating rituals based on the story of the Earth and the theology of creation to emerge from it. This search for appropriate rituals could spark a new period of creativity among Christians in music, art, dance and sacred texts.

Over and over again I have insisted that the story of the cosmos is one of fruitfulness, bountifulness and self-giving love. I do not however subscribe to the sedate, tamed vision of nature often associated with the Baroque and Romantic periods of European art and literature. There is a terrifying dimension to the story of Earth. The stars are born and sustained in violent transformations; so were the seas and land. While writing this book the ground beneath me here in South Cotabato has swayed ever so gently. In August 1976 it shook with a violent wrenching that left thousands of people dead. The long history of wars is a sad testimony to the fact that this dimension of terror is also evident in human individuals and cultures. In our day that threatening dimension is evident in the dropping of the atomic bomb on Hiroshima on 6 August 1945. This event and, I would argue, the cumulative impact of ecological destruction, point to our new found ability to extinguish the flame of life on this planet. Many of us tend to live as if this evil does not exist. We banish it into our subconscious where it haunts and disturbs us in a thousand ways.

We need powerful rituals to help us to face and wrestle with this evil. Tribal religions can give us a creative lead here. In almost every tribal society the central religious person is the shaman. He or she has a special sensitivity to the world of the spirits. Through the ability to enter into a trance the shaman can journey to the spirit world and there wrestle with the forces of evil on behalf of either an individual or the community. Very often the ensuing battle is won at great psychic cost before the shaman returns with healing and blessings. Almost every culture reflects this dynamic in the journey stories of its mythic hero doing battle with and defeating the dragon or the forces of evil symbolized in other ways. We are in dire need of such rituals today. Maybe a creative liturgy on this theme could be celebrated each year on 6 August – seeing that already there are celebrations to mark this black day – which holds the possibility of an even blacker day for all of us unless we truly wrestle with this devil and banish him. (I use the masculine pronoun since even the name of the bomb – Big Boy – has a masculine connotation.)

The liturgies I am suggesting here could provide a moment each year when a community could take stock of how it was husbanding the land, air, water, animal, insect and bird life with which God has blessed it. An individual and collective examination of conscience might be in order, to evaluate how people use scarce resources, especially energy. Do the members of that society use energy and natural resources wisely? Some estimate that the US, with only six percent of the world's population, uses forty percent of the world's primary resources. Are the rivers and seas being polluted? Are the farming methods burning out and destroying the fertility of the land in a single generation? Is the air being contaminated by industrial and domestic pollution and car emissions? Is the society addicted to fast foods or processed foods? Does the food eaten, such as grain-fed beef, consume large amounts of energy? Do people eat luxury fruits that are grown on Third–World land? Are the people creating mountains of non-biodegradable junk? The list could be extended depending on particular circumstances.

Another avenue is to ritualize some of the special ecological challenges facing a community. At Santa Cruz Mission we are trying to develop liturgies which draw on the cultural and religious experience of the people, the mystery of Christ and the challenges facing the community. These liturgies have been developed only during the past few years. A lot more experimentation is needed for more meaningful liturgies to emerge.

The loss of land through both legal and fraudulent means and the loss of soil fertility are the central, life or death, problems facing these people. At Santa Cruz Mission in South Cotabato in the Philippines we have endeavoured to devise a comprehensive programme to tackle these problems. To round off this programme with its integrated approach to a people's culture, and especially to the unique problems facing them today, it was felt that an Earth Liturgy, which follows below, would capture and celebrate many of their aspirations and struggles.

In recent years the Earth Liturgy has been celebrated during the second or third month of the year. It is better to have it some time before the planting season. This liturgy is best celebrated in a suitable house in the community, not in a church or in a small chapel. These latter are always associated in the minds of tribal people with lowland religion. In most communities the most spacious house is owned by the *Datu* (leader). Unless there are problems with his leadership in the community, the liturgy is celebrated there. The participants are encouraged to take some soil from their gardens, place it in a bamboo container and bring it along to the Liturgy.

The Earth Liturgy

Entrance   In T'boli culture gongs are always used to welcome guests, so the gongs are played while the people enter. As they do, the participants pour their soil into the earthen container in the centre of the house.

Introduction

(The leader introduces the theme.)
The Lord God made Earth
All life springs from it
All life returns to it.
God, Creator of the wide Earth (*talaktonok*),
you have given to every tribe and people their own territory.

To the T'boli you have given these mountains, forests, water and especially the land to support our plants, animals, children and ourselves.

Let us never lose our love for our Land, which is our mother. Help us to protect our soil from the hard-hearted man who would abuse her and from the intruder who would take our inheritance from us. Help us also to regain the land we have lost, to enrich soil which we have exhausted. Make our mother – The Earth – fruitful again.

Our own culture gives us a beautiful account of how the Earth was formed.

T'boli Creation Story In the beginning there were no mountains on Earth. As far as the eye could see, the water was spread out in all direction. The *D'wata* (the spirit) said 'I will create land for all the creatures so that they will have a place to live.' *D'wata* asked the hawk to find soil. Though he travelled a great distance over the oceans he could not find it. Then *D'wata* approached the dove and asked her. The dove flew continuously for eight days but even she failed to find soil. Lastly *D'wata* turned to the *Betoti* – a small, swift flying bird – and asked him. Before setting out on his adventure the *Betoti* left this message. 'If I return in eight days it means that I have seen soil. If, however, I do not return for sixteen days it means that something evil has happened to me.' The *Betoti* was lucky and found soil, so he placed some under his wing and returned within the eight days to *D'wata*.

Betoti carried very little soil. *D'wata* said to him, 'we will have to spread out the soil so that the waters can recede. Each place where you hop will become dry land.' For eight days and eight nights *Betoti* hopped backwards and forwards until after the eight days half the world was covered with land. Although he was exhausted *Betoti* was very happy with what he had achieved. He exclaimed 'How wonderful it is to have a place to stay. Let all the snakes, pigs, horses, carabaos and other animals, live in this place.'

So the animals moved to that place and began to live there. After a while one of the animals suggested to *Betoti* that they should have someone to look after them. Then *Betoti* formed sixteen clay statues, eight male and eight female. As he was forming them *Betoti* wondered how he could make them move or speak. *D'wata* knew this and he assured *Betoti* that he would help. After eight days one of the male statues moved. *Betoti* was very happy. He helped the man to walk, but he could not get him to speak for eight days. The first words of the man were 'What a privilege it is to be called to care for the Earth and the Sky.' Though he could move and speak, the man thought to himself, 'I am not content merely to watch over the animals. I must look for a suitable companion.' At that moment the female statue moved and she became man's partner and companion...

Responsorial Hymn
Response: Lord bless our land and your children who live by it.
Reader: How beautiful is the soil the Lord has made! It is rich and black and fruitful. A single seed planted in her womb will produce a hundred seeds. How beautiful is the soil the Lord has made.
Response: Lord bless our land and your children who live by it.
Reader: Who can live without soil? Can the carabao eat grass without soil? Can the wild pig survive without rooting in the soil of the forest? Even the eagle who soars above the highest mountain must return to the Earth to find food.
Response: Lord bless our land and your children who live by it.
Reader: When the Lord made humankind, He stooped down and took up Earth and shaped man and woman. He blew His breath upon the Earthen figures, and gave them His spirit. When the Lord made humankind, immediately He planted a garden for them.
Response: Lord bless our land and your children who live by it.
Reader: How precious is our soil, the gift above all gifts. Our soil is truly our Mother, A mother that contains us and feeds us. A child loves her mother. How precious is the soil, the gift above all gifts.

Sermon   The leader guides a community reflection on the importance of preserving their lands and looking after them. Land in the Bible is seen as God's gift to his people. They show their gratitude by not selling it or mortgaging it or allowing it to become eroded. The notes supplied with the liturgical text also call attention to the respect for the spirit of the land, forest and mountains found in the traditional culture and the need to strengthen that or recapture it, if it has been lost.

Common Prayers   The prayer leader, and anyone else who wishes to do so, prays for the needs of the community, especially those relating to the land.

Blessing The Soil   The leader stands over the earthen pot, into which the people have poured the soil at the beginning of the service, and pronounces a prayer of blessing on all the farms in the area.
Guide: God, Our Father and Mother, bless this Earth which we have brought here from our (*teniba*) farms. You have given us the Earth as our Mother. Make it rich and fruitful so that it may nourish all creatures, especially your children. By this holy water which we now sprinkle make fruitful our soil. Let it always bring forth life.

Litany of the Plants   Two groups of chanters sing a litany of praise for many of the plants found in T'boli environment. When the liturgy was being devised an effort was made to include many traditional plants which have almost vanished from the area. This proved to be one of the most memorable aspects of the liturgy. Many old people cried when plants which have become extinct were recalled.
Reader: For our *halay kenumay* and our *halay teng* (traditional varieties of rice)
Response: Let the Earth bring forth life!
Reader: For our *k'leb* and *ubi koyu* ... (traditional varieties of root crops)
Response: Let the Earth bring forth life!
Reader: For our *t'wol* and *tule* ... (traditional fruits)

Response: Let the Earth bring forth life!
Reader: For our *blanqui* and *buli* ... (traditional vegetables)
Response: Let the Earth bring forth life!
Reader: For *kolon* and *fet* ... (traditional grasses)
Response: Let the Earth bring forth life!
Reader: For our *mangga* and *bekadu* ... (more recently introduced fruits)
Response: Let the Earth bring forth life!
Reader: For our *kenalum* and *loco* ... (varieties of trees)
Response: May the Earth bring forth life!
Guide: Father in heaven we thank you for the Earth that you have given to us and for all the blessings of life which you have showered upon us. In your goodness we ask you to let the soil bring forth an abundance of life to nourish the whole community of the living and to renew your children in body and spirit.

Kifil Tau Nedung (Moulding a clay figurine)
During this part of the ceremony, the leader pours water into the earthen jar and moulds the Earth into the form of a human figure. He or she then places the earthen figure in the centre of the earthen jar.
Guide: My friends, we have blessed this soil and have prayed to God that He will make it fruitful for all our plants and animals. We know that God made humankind from the soil. In order that we do not forget this let us make a *tau medung* (human figurine).
Guide: When God made the Earth and planted it with every kind of plant, He made all the animals that crawl on the ground, all the animals that run in the fields, the birds that fly through the air, and the fish that swim in the rivers and lakes. And when all was prepared God formed humankind from the soil. God shaped them with His own fingers and blew His breath into them to give them life.

Kelunol Tonok be Uyo (Placing Earth on the forehead of the participants)
Guide: My friends you understand that after our lives

here on Earth our bodies must return to the Earth, to remain there until they awaken on the Last Day. Though our spirits live on, when we die, our bodies return to the Earth that once gave us life.

(At this point the guide presses the Earth figure into the Earth in the jar to symbolize that we return to the Earth)
Guide: Now let us sign our foreheads with soil as a sign that we have come from Earth and must return to her.

(The guide and the assistants place the soil in the form of a cross on the foreheads of all present.)
Guide: Remember you are from the soil and that you will return to her.

Final Prayer   O God, Creator of this beautiful Earth which you have filled with abundance of living creatures. Help us never to forget that our life and the life of every creature depends upon our soil. Help us to be always grateful for this most precious gift. Enrich our soil, make it black and fruitful and rich. Protect us from long periods of drought and floods. Bless our land, especially your People.

Dismissal and Final Ritual   My friends, today we are marked again with the sign of the Earth. May the Earth from which we come and to which we must return be always before our eyes. May we be grateful to God for her and respect her as Mother when we return to our farms. (At this point everyone goes out from the house and the earthen jug containing the blessed Earth is also brought out. Then the *soyow* is danced. The *soyow* is a very special dance in T'boli culture. It is normally performed during the most important traditional feast which is called the *Mo Ninum*. The *soyow* is both a territorial dance and celebration of fertility so it is very appropriate as a concluding rite for this celebration. After the *soyow* is completed the blessed Earth is distributed so that the participants may scatter it on their farms.)

Other liturgies prepared by the Santa Cruz Mission staff celebrate other gifts within the natural world. A *Water Liturgy* recognizes water as the universal source of life and asks God to bless the water sources in each community. The responsorial hymn calls to mind the joy and refreshment which people associate with water as they bathe in a clear stream or slake their thirst in sparkling spring water. The congregation responds with a cry of praise:

Tey tilob el tikaw How beautiful fresh water is
Salamat Bong D'wata Thanks to our Great Spirit.

The sermon notes, to guide the sharing, speak of water in the Bible. Through water and the Spirit the Christian is reborn. This is very symbolic for the T'boli community. Baptism is normally only administered once a year during the Easter Vigil. The catechumens are all baptized in the local river called the *Lowo-el*. During the Water Liturgy the people are challenged to take care of the springs and water sources. In many tropical countries, water-borne diseases are one of the main causes of infant mortality and other illnesses. The relationship between the forest and the water sources is also called to mind.

After the sharing and community prayers, the head of each family pours water from their particular water source into an earthenware jar. The guide or prayer leader then blesses the water. After the blessing the water is sprinkled on the congregation. This is followed by a litany of praise for water and all the creatures found in the waters. After the final blessing each family pours some holy water back into its bamboo container and carries it back to their well. The final part of the ceremony takes place at the well. The family makes a traditional offering or *demsu*. This is done by placing some valuable objects like a betel nut box, a traditional sword or a long tunic-type garment called a *l'wek* near the spring to involve the blessing of the spirit of the well on all the people.

A *Fire Liturgy* gives thanks to God for the gift of fire. Fire is the original 'stuff' of the cosmos and fire is one of the most significant milestones in the story of human history. The liturgy calls to mind the purifying and transformative power of fire which invites the community to be transformed itself by the fire of Christian love. The liturgy also speaks of the danger of fire so the community is exhorted not to be careless with this gift. Forest fires in 1983 caused untold damage to tropical forests in the Philippines. Burning vegetation instead of composting it wastes organic matter and can lead to major fires. This liturgy ends with a prayer, which is of concern to all humankind, that God will spare his world and his people from being incinerated in the fireball of a nuclear holocaust.

These liturgies centred on natural symbols have now been in use for a number of years. It is not possible to give a thorough evaluation of their impact. I have, however, participated in them in a number of different communities. When they are prepared beforehand and conducted with care, the people seem to enter deeply into the celebration. Hopefully, they will stimulate other communities to create liturgies which are appropriate for their own aspirations and challenges.

10

CELEBRATING SACRAMENTS OF LIFE

There is no attempt here to present a systematic sacramental theology, or even a theology of individual sacraments. A wealth of books and articles has appeared in recent years which treat the scriptural, theological, psychological, sociological and anthropological dimensions of the sacraments. The goal of this short presentation is to heighten our awareness of a single dimension of sacramental praxis today. The sacraments are always celebrated in a particular time and place. They engage men and women living in particular communities with concrete aspirations and yearnings. One of these, experienced in ever-widening circles today, is concern for the Earth. The celebration of the sacraments provides the Christian community with many opportunities for celebrating the gift of the natural world, and developing an ecologically sensitive catechesis.

Our reflections on the sacraments go beyond the possibilities they afford for ecological catechesis. In the last chapter, I called attention to what anthropologists and sociologists today are telling us about the inseparable bond between a particular reality and what it symbolizes. If the connection with ordinary, everyday experiences is broken, then the range of symbolic possibilities which formerly could be taken for granted, may well be hampered, and in some cases destroyed. In what follows I will question whether the deteriorating quality of the natural world weakens the symbolic impact of the sacrament. Does the fact that there seems to be an increasingly worldwide shortage of clean water mean that water will no longer be a powerful symbol of renewal and new life in the sacrament of Baptism?

The same applies to the Eucharist. Does the widespread hunger, malnutrition, unequal distribution of food, together with destruction of cropland, plant species and genetic variety, lessen the symbolic power of bread or food to be an effective symbol for the Bread of Life? Is an important dimension missing in the sacrament of reconciliation, if harmony with the Earth is not included? Marriage celebrates human love and fruitfulness. Is the rapid increase in the human population, especially in some areas of the world, destroying countless other species in the Earth community and, consequently, endangering the health of the total community?

Baptism

Water is the central symbol in the sacrament of Baptism. St Paul in Romans 6:3–4 speaks of being baptized into Christ: 'Have you forgotten that when we were baptized into union with Christ Jesus we were baptized into his death? By Baptism we were buried with him, and lay in death, in order that as Christ was raised from the dead in the splendour of the Father, so also we might set our feet upon the new path of life.'

Here the symbol of water has a two-fold thrust. It symbolizes the cleansing, purifying effect of Baptism for the individual. More importantly still, it symbolizes new life. Going down into the waters and experiencing death to sin is a prelude to rising with Christ to new life. We are renewed and transformed by the paschal mystery of Christ, and, in the process, we are incorporated into the community of believers where we will live and celebrate this new life. This symbolic power is possible because water is universally experienced by human beings in at least three ways: as the source of life, as a means for purification or cleansing, and as an instrument of death, through drowning.

Since the beginning of the Christian era, theologians could take for granted that the water in its natural condition – rain, snow, running streams, lakes and oceans – was fresh, clean and life-giving. A book by Fred Powledge entitled *Water: The Nature, Uses and Future of our Most Precious and Abused Resource*[1] questions whether this assumption is still true. Much of the data, which I presented in my discussion of the polluted condition of water, both worldwide and in Ireland, raises the very same question. If the purity of water continues to deteriorate, will it still retain the power to symbolize new life and purification? This fear of destroying the symbolic power of water and other natural symbols should act as another spur to Christians to be particularly concerned about what is happening to our most precious resources. If the natural water systems, for example, are poisoned, water will come to symbolize death with no regenerative power. How can it then be an effective symbol for the transformative power of the life, death and resurrection of Jesus?

Eucharist

Much of what was said above in relation to Baptism also applies today in any serious discussion of the Eucharist. St John in chapter 6 of his Gospel, and the Church through the centuries, presented the Eucharist as the Bread of Life. If the Eucharist symbolizes food and drink and sharing a meal in the memory of Jesus, who lived, died and rose from the dead, the most important challenge facing any celebration of the Eucharist today is not the legitimacy of the priest's orders, or the appropriateness of the liturgical text, but the fact that the Eucharist is today celebrated in a world where over one thousand million people are regularly hungry.

Hunger, malnutrition, lack of opportunities to grow and harvest food, the erosion of the genetic base of our staple foods, the control of seeds by a few giant companies and the continual degradation of fertile croplands are all interrelated. One cannot celebrate the Eucharist today without being challenged to do something about this appalling reality. This point is eloquently made in a talk by the then superior-general of the Jesuits, Pedro Arrupe, entitled *Hunger for Bread and Evangelization*, at the Eucharistic Congress in Philadelphia in 1974:

> If there is hunger anywhere in the world then our celebration of the Eucharist is somehow incomplete everywhere in the world. He comes to us not alone, but with the poor, the oppressed, the starving of the Earth. Through Him they are looking to us for help, for justice, for love expressed in action. Therefore we cannot properly receive the Bread of Life unless at the same time we give bread for life to those in need, wherever, whoever they may be.[2]

Hunger in 1986 is worse than it was in 1974. In 1974, at the time of the World Food Conference in Rome, the United Nations estimated that 460 million people were permanently hungry and suffering from the disease and misery that malnutrition brings in its wake. By 1984 the figure had jumped to over 1,000 million according to the Director of the FAO (Food and Agricultural Organization). This staggering figure – nearly a quarter of the human race regularly suffering from the pangs of hunger and serious malnutrition – cries to heaven for vengeance in a world where over a million dollars is spent every minute on the military. It certainly heightens the prophetic challenge of celebrating the Eucharist in First-World countries. Each Eucharist, in which we receive the Bread of Life, should challenge our society to ask why it is that so much of our resources is dedicated to weapons of death when there is so much hunger.

Given this blight of hunger on the face of the Earth, one would think that First–World nations, particularly the traditionally Christian countries of Europe and North America, would marshal their enormous resources to eliminate poverty. Combating poverty has always generated a certain amount of political rhetoric in the West. President Kennedy set twin goals for the US in the early 1960s. One was to put a man on the moon; this was achieved by 1970. The second was to combat and conquer hunger; the situation in many Third-World countries, in fact, deteriorated during the 1960s. Henry Kissinger repeated the same pledge at the Rome Conference in 1974. Eleven years later the number of hungry people continues to grow at a frightening rate. In the intervening years, western countries have often stood idly by and even benefited from other people's hunger.

Natural calamities like long droughts or severe floods are often the immediate cause of famine in many Third-World countries, but the long-term cause is directly linked to the economic and trading policies of western nations. In 1973, the oil embargo and quadrupling of oil prices created a furore in Western countries and in the media, because of the major impact of this decision on western countries. The previous year the United States sold 19 million tonnes of wheat to the USSR. This trading decision was a crushing blow to starving people everywhere. It resulted in the tripling of grain prices which, in turn, sent other food prices spiralling. Poor countries that were forced to import food could not meet their food bill; the US on the other hand benefited. It registered a $13 billion dollar increase in farm exports between 1972 and 1974.

I have already called attention to the fact that the prime land in many Third-World countries is used by transnational corporations to grow food and produce beef for First-World markets. During a visit to the Philippines in 1979, Lappe and McCallie[3] found that 57,000 hectares of arable land, previously devoted to food for local consumption, had in a period of ten years been converted to export-oriented fruit farms. I was very much aware of this during the famine in Mindanao in 1983. A seven-month drought caused extensive crop failure, especially in areas where there was no irrigation or where irrigation canals had dried up. Many tribal peoples and poor lowlands peasants were constantly hungry to the point of starvation. Yet in the midst of this hunger, land in the province of South Cotabato was devoted to growing pineapples for export to First-World countries.

The response of western nations to the famine that affected 29 countries and threatened 50 million people in Africa in 1984 was extremely slow. Though the dire situation of the people was well-known to western governments, they chose to ignore it. In fact, some took financial decisions which guaranteed that the cycle of poverty, famine and desertification would continue elsewhere. In the spring of 1984, for example, just when the first glimpses of the catastrophe were beginning to appear in the western media, the Reagan administration announced that it was cutting back, to the tune of $3 billion, on its lending to the International Development Association – an agency which provides cheap capital to poor developing countries. Without pressure from the media, western governments would have let Africa starve.

The proportions of the famine, especially in Ethiopia, only finally came home to westerners after a BBC television team toured the area. Questions were raised whether both the Reagan administration and the Thatcher government had deliberately adopted a low profile because of the fact that a Marxist government was in power in Addis Ababa. Western governments tried to exonerate themselves from blame by highlighting the corruption and incompetence within Ethiopia and pointing to the fact that the West was doing more than the USSR and its allies.

One staggering anomaly of our times is that, while the famine in Africa is taking a heavy toll on the Earth and on human lives, many western countries have huge food surpluses. The EEC has mountains of butter, beef, lamb, pork and sugar, and lakes of milk and wine. Australia has mountains of wheat. The cost of storing and preserving this growing surplus is enormous, yet, because of the impact it would have on the farm prices and incomes, the EEC and Australia cannot make this food available to hungry people.

By the latter part of 1984, western governments and private and Church relief organizations were attempting to bring food, medical help and shelter to people in East Africa. The appeal for help struck responsive chords in many people's hearts. School children, trade-union groups and a wide variety of people have contributed generously to appeals for help. A group of popular musicians got together to produce a disc to help the relief drive. While this crisis intervention is absolutely essential in order to keep people alive, it will eventually prove useless unless the land is rehabilitated also.

Drought is the proximate cause of famine in Ethiopia. The long-term cause is ecological damage through overgrazing, tree-felling and cultivating land which is unsuitable for agriculture. In this way thousands of acres of land are lost each year to encroaching sands and deserts. So the problem of a deteriorating environment is intimately linked to famine. Real concern for the First-World must go beyond meeting the present crisis to providing the capital and expertise which will help break the vicious circle which links growing poverty to a deteriorating environment.

Private and government funding and relief agencies are not overly receptive to this message, as I learned from experience during the famine in Mindanao in 1983. Money to feed the hungry slowly seeped through, but the request for capital to reclaim farm land and make it productive again fell on deaf ears. It was also in the context of the 1983 famine that I began to understand the Eucharistic dimension of what was happening to the land in Mindanao. If the land becomes barren, through human neglect or as a result of unjust economic policies, then it will not provide nourishment for our bodies or spirits.

Our experience of sharing the Bread of Life should provide the motivation for Christians in the West to tackle the problems of world hunger, poverty, and deteriorating environment. These have reached crisis proportions for everyone on Earth. Ultimately the survival of everyone may depend on whether we reverse the ecological destruction which goes hand-in-hand with widespread poverty.

This is the theme of the following 'Parable of the Bad Neighbours' by William Clarke which appeared in *The Tablet* in February 1984. It raises the possibility that, in our obsession with achieving military superiority in order to feel secure, we may be myopic. The Achilles heel for both the eastern European countries and the NATO block may not be the lack of another more sophisticated weapons-system. Both already have enough nuclear weapons to destroy the world a number of times over. Rather, the collapse of our present civilization may come from the destruction of the Earth by poor hungry people struggling to survive for one more day. Their scavenging may endanger the future for everyone because damage to the Earth endangers everyone.

Two families moved into a semi-detached house with a rather thin dividing wall, which permitted them to hear, but not understand, everything that went on in the other's abode. Both families became convinced that the other was attempting to break through the wall, and murder them in their beds. So they each built up a battery of alarm signals, and more and more sophisticated booby traps and explosive devices, which would enable them utterly to destroy the neighbours if they ever attempted to break through.

The cost of their burglar proofing was so great that neither family had any cash to spare to fix up the cellar and basement. There, in damp, overcrowded squalor, a large number of poor coloured tenants lived. In the mid-winter the basement became so cold that the tenants used their axes to chop off bits of the joist in their ceiling to build fires to keep warm. Messages came from upstairs forbidding them to shake the building, lest the alarm systems were activated and everyone blown up: But as a concession, upstairs did promise to turn up the electric heating so that some warmth would trickle downstairs! But heat does not trickle down. So the blacks quietly and carefully sawed away the wood. After a time the joists gave way, the floor sank, the dividing wall tottered and fell, thus exploding all its defensive devices and killing everyone on both sides of the building.

The main thrust of the discussion here is that adequate food, justice for people and the continued fruitfulness of the Earth are interrelated. They are the most pressing problems facing the world during the last decades of the twentieth century. The Christian virtue of hospitality binds these concerns together. Matthew's Gospel tells us that any discussion about the Eucharist or attempt to live out the Christian message that does not respond to the hungry is at variance with the works of Jesus: 'For when I was hungry, you gave me food; when thirsty you gave me drink (Matt. 25:35)'. Matthew Fox[4] insists that the hospitality symbolized by the Eucharistic banquet is a cosmic hospitality. It is an opportunity to give thanks for all of God's blessings. The bread and wine which become the Body and Blood of Christ unite us and him to all creation, so that each Eucharist should be a challenge to us to change political and economic structures which enslave huge segments of humanity and destroy the Earth.

Reconciliation

It seems to me that the Catholic Church let slip a golden opportunity to pursue actively the theme of reconciliation with the Earth at the 1983 Synod of Bishops on Reconciliation and Penance. Many psychologists would agree with Eric Fromm that much of the debilitating anxiety experienced by modern men and women springs from three sources: their alienation from themselves, particularly their bodies, their lack of a genuine sense of human community and, finally, their alienation from nature. Any genuine reconciliation would have to include these dimensions of human alienation.

The anthropology underlying much of the official Church's approach to reconciliation overlooks any real relationship between what is happening to the Earth and the injustice, oppression and sinfulness in human relations. Even though Rachel Carson's book *Silent Spring* was published in 1962, the Fathers of the Second Vatican Council had nothing to say about the destruction of the Earth outside the context of nuclear war; *Gaudium et Spes* condemns 'any act of war aimed indiscriminately at the destruction of entire cities or of extensive areas, along with their population as a crime against God and man himself'.[5] The bishops did not see that the destruction being brought about by acid rain, industrial, agricultural, human, nuclear and chemical pollution will also sterilize the planet, though the time-scale may be a little longer. That hardly makes it any less destructive or offensive to people who celebrate life.

In the intervening years since the Council, a wealth of data and reflection has been published by individual scientists, national and international ecological and conservation agencies and the United Nations, pointing out that disaster is looming unless something is done soon. Still, none of the major Christian Churches, including the Catholic Church, has issued a comprehensive document of encyclical proportions to help Christians understand the deep roots of the problem, to challenge religious people to change their life-style and consumption patterns and care for the Earth in a more active way as part of their living out of the Christian mysteries.

The Synod on Reconciliation (1983) would appear to have been ideal for developing such a stance, given the theme of the Synod, and the fact that the bishops came from all over the world. The *Lineamenta* (the preliminary discussion papers)[6] published about a year before the Synod were not very promising. When it spoke about the world, the Synod focused exclusively on the human, thus excluding about ninety-nine percent of the Earth community. As I pointed out during the discussion of redemption, when the Earth dimension is excluded from any reflection on sin and redemption, both sin and reconciliation are trivialized. The stance men and women take towards the Earth is of a piece with their stance towards their fellow human beings. If their approach to the Earth is marked by lack of respect, arrogance, greed and rapaciousness, then they will also oppress and exploit their brothers and sisters if the opportunity presents itself. If, through a true conversion of heart, they seek a harmonious relationship with nature and show respect, love and gratitude for all of creation, this will also spill over into their human affairs and transform their relationships.

The *Lineamenta* did not seem to realize this. The Synod itself was also disappointing. While many bishops pushed the horizons beyond the narrow confines of the preparatory documents to include discussion on the arms race, racial and religious discrimination and oppression of millions of people by totalitarian regimes of the right or left, very few speakers drew attention to the destruction of the environment. Having checked through the summaries of the bishops' interventions provided in *L'Osservatore Romano*, I found only one speech which adverted to this important dimension of reconciliation. I think it is significant that the only contribution on this theme that I saw was from a Japanese bishop. Japan has developed over the centuries one of the most aesthetic cultures in human history. It also is the only country to date to experience the hell of nuclear explosions. The summary of Bishop Stephen Fumio Hamao's intervention reads as follows:

Work for peace will be effective if all men become aware
of their deep connection with nature, especially with all
living beings. Man must not only dominate nature, but
also seek harmony with it and admire in it the beauty,
wisdom and love of its Creator. Thus men will be freed
from their frenzy for possessions and domination and will
become artisans for peace. (10 October 1983)

Unfortunately, the intervention must not have made much
impact on the Synod Fathers. There is no mention of the
environment in the message published at the conclusion of the
Synod. Sad to say, this lack of sensitivity to the need for
reconciliation with the Earth is also found in the post-Synodal
Apostolic Exhortation, *Reconciliatio et Paenitentia*, which was
published in December of 1984.[7]

Marriage and the Family

In marriage, the love of husband and wife is expressed in a
unique way in sexual intercourse. Here according to the
Genesis account of creation the two become 'one flesh' (Gen.
2:24). In recent years there has been a flowering in the
theology of marriage. Many of the more important insights
have come from married people reflecting on their own
experience. One important gain in the recent theological and
scriptural writings on marriage is that it has unshackled the
Roman Catholic Church from a negative view of sexuality and
marriage, which owes much more to the influence of
neo-Platonism than to the biblical tradition. The fruitful love
between husband and wife manifests itself in a special way in
the procreation and rearing of children. This is a symbol of
God's love for human beings and all creation. It is also a most
profound statement that the couple actually believe in a future
for their children and their children's children – that the world
will continue to nurture and nourish human beings. So in the
sacrament of marriage the couple are involved not merely in
the mystery of human or Earth fertility but in the loving
relationship between God and all creation. Hildegarde dwells
on this in her writings: 'I compare the love of creature and
creation to the same love and fidelity with which God binds

men and women together. This is so that together they might be creatively fruitful.'[8]

The inner dynamics of true love draws a couple on beyond the bounds of concern for themselves, or even for their children or the local community in which they live. Though these dynamics are rooted in all these relationships, fruitful love carries the couple beyond them all to embrace the totality of creation. This love and care for creation strengthens and enriches all other relations because all things are connected. Ultimately, the couple's own health and well-being, the well-being of their children and the whole human community depends on the well-being of the Earth. A sick planet will wound every being on the planet. For the Christian couple, their 'yes' in marriage becomes a 'yes' to God, to each other to their children and community and finally to the Earth.

The study of the fertility of the family and ecology are closely related. On page 17 we saw that *oikos* was derived from the Greek word for family-household. Today many ecologists and demographers are worried that the human family is growing too quickly and placing demands on the Earth which are damaging irreparably its continual fruitfulness. The situation is particularly worrying in many Third-World countries. Modern medicine has helped reduce infant mortality and the death rate among young children, so that their populations are composed predominantly of young dependents who will themselves be having families within a few short years.

The population profile in First-World countries is very different. There, life expectancy is now in the mid to high seventies and, with extensive practice of birth control and high living standards, births and deaths balance each other. In many First-World countries there is a stable population, while in a number of countries like Germany and Denmark the population is expected to decline by the year 2000. It is interesting to note that Ireland has a high birth rate for a First-World country. The population is expected to increase by 17.5 percent by the year 2000.

Despite the decline in population in a number of countries, the overall world population is increasing at a rapid rate. Some understanding of the increase over the past 10,000 years might help to put what is happening today in perspective. It is estimated that 10,000 years ago there were only between eight and ten million people on Earth. During Jesus's life-time the number had increased to 250 million. In 1650 there were about 850 million, yet the one billion mark was not reached until 1850. Since then the doubling time has decreased significantly. The two billion mark was passed in the 1930s. In 1984 the world population was estimated at 4.6 billion, with one billion now being added each decade. It is expected to continue to rise until the early part of the twenty-first century. Some experts project that the world population by 2000 will be over six billion, and that it might reach as high as eleven billion before levelling off.

This dramatic contemporary rise in population is almost exclusively a Third-World phenomenon. The increase is taking place in countries with the least food resources, housing, medical or educational facilities to deal with it. In the Philippines, for example, the population has doubled almost four times since the beginning of the century, from a little over four million to 54.9 million today. Mercedes Conception, the Dean of the University of the Philippines' Population Institute, told a Population Welfare Conference in Manila in August 1984 that according to present projections the population will reach over 70 million by the year 2000 – just sixteen years away.

Third-World cities are the fastest growing areas. Today over seven million people are crowded into Manila, many of them living in slums and shanty towns. By the year 2005, the population is expected to jump to sixteen million. Mexico City, for example, had 1.5 million people in 1940. By 1960 the number has climbed to 2.7 million. In 1984 it was 14 million and even with successful family planning programmes it is estimated to reach at least 25 million by the year 2000. The figures for Sao Paulo are much the same. In 1940 the population was 1.3 million. The projected population for the year 2000 is 20.8 million.[9] How the majority of people can hope to have any kind of satisfying human life among such congestion baffles the imagination.

A simple statistical approach to the problem of population might suggest that a massive birth control compaign is the only viable solution. Given the magnitude of the problem it is understandable why many population conferences and semi-nars have opted for this approach, particularly in view of the phenomenal rate of increase in numerous Third-World cities.

In response to these figures, extensive birth control measures were advocated by many First-World countries at the Population Conference in Bucharest in 1974. Needless to say, the Third-World delegates, though aware of their problems, did not respond very favourably to this suggestion. In fact, they saw the western advice, especially when tied to western aid, as neocolonialism, and reacted with anger. They also pointed out that in spite of the fact that the First-World only contains one third of the world's population their people consume eighty percent of the Earth's resources.

The need for a more equitable distribution of the Earth's resources is an important element in discussing population increase. People are not poor because they have large families. In fact it is the other way around. When poverty and unequal access to resources are endemic, poor people tend to have large families to ensure that at least some members of the family will survive, become bread winners and care for the parents in their old age. Here justice is once again linked to ecological concerns. A more just distribution of the world's resources and more equitable trade and exchange terms will hasten an end to poverty, malnutrition, infant mortality and disease. History teaches us that when this happens fertility declines.

Any serious consideration of the population issue must stress the primary importance of economic, social and ecological progress. It is utopian to think that this, however, will be achieved without extensive family planning. Take Kenya as an example. A GNP growth rate of six percent for the first decade after independence was cancelled out by the rapid growth in population taking place at the same time. After the oil price increase in the early seventies the GNP slumped to three percent, but the population continued to grow at much the same rate. In 1980 the population was 17 million. By the year 2000 that is projected to grow to 40 million and a quarter of a century later to 83 million. All the economic pointers indicate that the country's ability to support the growing population is diminishing rather than increasing. The country has a huge foreign debt. Imports, especially oil, have jumped ten times, while the income from exports has remained constant. Most important of all, many question whether the carrying capacity of the local biological systems can support such a population in both the near- and long-term future.

Many governments recognizing this dilemma have introduced birth control programmes gently, at first on a non-coercive basis, but quickly more coercive measures such as forced sterilization and abortion are resorted to. This coercion, in such a delicate area of human affairs, sometimes causes a backlash. The fall of Mrs Indira Gandhi's government in 1977 is a case in point. In criticizing birth control programmes in any country the Catholic Church provides two important services. Along with other institutions, it strengthens human freedom when it decries the degrading or inhuman methods proposed for family planning. The second service is to continue to insist that birth control divorced from land reform and other bio-regional development projects is an oppressive tool in the hands of the rich.

Having said that, I thank that the official Catholic Church must recognize the dilemmas involved, and begin to take seriously the rapid world-wide increase in population and the catastrophe which faces many countries unless there is a significant fall in the birth rate. Even though there has been a decline in the birth rate in the Philippines in recent years, the population is still expected to double within twenty-eight years. Today the Philippines has one of the highest malnutrition rates in Asia. How is the country which, as we saw in Chapter 2, is rapidly exhausting its natural system, going to feed 108 million within 30 years and 216 within 60 years?

These are serious questions, but it seems to me that Catholic leaders do not wish to think seriously about them in case they may appear to be challenging the teaching of *Humanae Vitae*. Local Church officials are content to sit idly by and procrastinate in face of a problem which threatens to destroy both human society and the total environment. An example of this paralysis came to my attention recently. In 1985 the bishops of the Philippines decided to draft a pastoral letter on Development Issues. Social, political and economic options were mentioned in the first draft, but not a word about the environment or the dramatic population increase.

It must be admitted, however, that the situation of the official Catholic Church is by no means simple. On the one hand the Church has done much to support research into natural family planning methods. This contribution to humanity should not be underestimated, as natural family planning methods have much to recommend them. Apart from being effective, they also promote and often enrich the love between husband and wife. Yet even here many of the people who promote these programmes are often frustrated by the fact that even natural family planning is not very high on the list of pastoral priorities.

In addition, these methods demand maturity, privacy, reasonable living standards and a co-operative relationship between husband and wife. This explains why generally they are more successful among middle-class people than among the poor. A paper published by John E. Laing, an associate of the Population Council,[10] shows that there has been an increase in the number of couples using the 'rhythm' method in the Philippines. However, even these do not have an accurate knowledge of what is involved and so there is a high failure rate.

On the other hand, many Catholics in First-World countries simply ignore the Church's doctrinal teaching on artificial methods and choose which methods they will use. The American bishops at the Synod of the Family in 1980 admitted that the percentage of Catholics in the US using artificial methods of birth control was roughly similar to that of other groups in the country. Many lay people in both First- and Third-World countries consider that the present position of the Church lacks credibility. Could it be the fact that the Church's spokesmen are almost invariably celibate males contributes to this opinion? Married people who are struggling with the problems of secular life feel that many bishops and priests have an unrealistic understanding of marriage. Clerics are cushioned against most of the economic problems like inflation and unemployment which are uppermost in lay people's minds.

Given the fact that rapid population increase, particularly in

Third-World countries, is one of the most serious problems facing the Earth community in our time, and that there are many genuine dilemmas involved in any response to the problems, Church leaders should encourage widespread debate in order to face the issues. Sad to say this is not the case. One's personal position *vis-à-vis Humanae Vitae* has become almost a litmus test for Catholic orthodoxy. Subtle, and not so subtle, pressures are used to silence those who promote the necessary debate and dialogue.

This lack of realism and commitment to face a serious problem is particularly evident in many Vatican officials. In a news item in *The Tablet*, 5 January 1985, Archbishop (now Cardinal) Edouard Gagnon alleges that 'the opposition to *Humanae Vitae* was above all orchestrated by certain professors to spread their own ideas about the autonomy of the individual conscience'. No doubt some professors who opposed *Humanae Vitae* sought support among their colleagues but to attribute the widespread practical dissent among married Catholics to plots among theology professors is to carry the conspiracy theory to ridiculous lengths. It greatly over-estimates the influence of theologians! The majority of Catholics who have decided to practise artificial methods of birth control have never read a book by a moral theologian!

To summarize what I have been saying in this chapter, the sacraments provide appropriate moments for the Christian community to reflect on what is happening to the natural world, since the symbolic power of all the sacraments is rooted there. The point at issue here is not merely that the sacraments provide an opportunity to respond to the aspirations of many Christians who today are concerned about the ecological crisis facing our world. It is that with the widespread destruction of the natural world the symbolic potential inherent in the Earth is impoverished. This aspect, especially, in relation to population also raises serious moral and ethical problems. Do individual human beings always, and in every situation, have priority over other creatures, even when a rapid increase in human population levels invariably involves the extinction of numerous species? Should the human population be kept at a level which will allow other species to survive? What ethical and moral norms should govern such policies? These complex questions lead us into the next chapter on the Christian response.

11

'THOU SHALT NOT KILL'

A New Moral Theology

The ecological perspective of the new story must also shed light on many moral and ethical questions. In order to be relevant to the problems of our times an ethical system today must have wider parameters than the ones found in the traditional manuals of ethics or moral theology. Very often traditional moral principles emerge from a static view of human beings and the world in which we live. This tradition emphasized absolute and immutable laws with little thought for the cultural, historical and ecological determinants or consequences of a particular action. Today moral theology and ethics need to be more comprehensive and dynamic. They must combine principles governing individual human behaviour, concern for social justice among disparate groups, a comprehensive approach to the natural world, and a concern for the ethics of the whole continuing evolutionary process.

Our ethical tradition has seen important developments in recent years. Until recently moral theology and ethics were focused almost exclusively on individual moral responsibility for inter-personal behaviour. Much less thought was given to the moral ramifications of group behaviour. Few moralists discussed the moral dimensions of social justice such as I have raised here. In the relationship between nations this would include, for example, the way First-World countries enjoy preferential access to the life-systems and resources of the Earth to the detriment of poorer countries; how the monetary and financial policies of 'developed' countries force 'developing' countries to use a large percentage of their export earnings to service their debts; how selective restrictions on trading between First- and Third-World countries ensure that Third-World countries will always be in a dependent and vulnerable position. The moral accountability of predominantly First-World institutions, such as multinational corporations, needs to be regularly assessed, especially if their economic and employment policies exploit workers and the environment in Third-World countries.

The attempts of moral theologians to identify group responsibility for evil is a return to an earlier strand of human moral experience which is found in the Old Testament, particularly in the Book of Judges, and in many tribal societies. Today, some moral theologians like Fr Bernard Häring[1] are beginning to broaden their parameters even further in order to include serious discussion of the way human beings relate to the Earth and to other creatures in the Earth community. The integrity, stability and ever-renewing capacity of the biotic community is now becoming the widest context for moral activity.

In 'The Parable of the Bad Neighbours' we saw how the over-consumption of the Earth's resources by people in capitalist and socialist countries is beggaring most of the world's people and ultimately endangering everyone. Our moral focus now needs to move beyond the impact of our actions on our contemporaries. In the final analysis, the behaviour of people today reaches into the future. Our current lack of respect for the Earth constitutes an injustice perpetrated against generations to come. They will be condemned to live within a damaged world, depleted of many natural resources. This introduces a new and, in a sense, ultimate dimension into the moral equation. It is not enough merely to look at inter-personal activity nor even at the impact of one group's behaviour on contemporaries. Moralists should now clarify the moral implications of what people do today on future generations so that we can have a real appreciation regarding the long-term effects of our actions. Our generation has a power which no previous generation had in history. We can literally destroy essential elements of creation. Today, human behaviour is involved with ultimate realities in a way unknown to previous generations. Nuclear war is the most immediate and dramatic illustration of this new potential but, although the time-scale will be longer, ecological deterioration will achieve the same results.

Given the seemingly unlimited power which nuclear, chemical and genetic technologies have put into the hands of this generation, we are faced with ultimate moral questions with which our tradition has hardly equipped us to deal. Our moral sensibilities have not kept pace with our technologies of destruction. One problem with our traditional Christian moral paradigm is that forgiveness is easy enough to obtain as long as one expresses one's sorrow and promises not to repeat the evil. The willingness to forgive, particularly in the context of inter-personal sins, is one of the strengths of the Judeo-Christian tradition. Today, however, when it is applied to the wider ecological frame, it has its obvious weaknesses.

A person may well be willing to forgive the perpetrator of an evil, but once the fabric of the Earth is destroyed, even if the culprit is forgiven, the cosmic harmony is much more difficult. to re-establish. A person may be genuinely sorry for leaking nuclear waste and wish to close down all nuclear plants. Nevertheless the damage caused will continue inexorably for thousands of years. Matthew Fox puts it well when he says:[2] 'the Cosmos keeps a ledger – not God; and cosmic order will not in the long run tolerate human greed, human indifference to its beauties and its laws of balance and harmony'.

He quotes a text from Hildegarde which is very apt in the context of the present discussion, 'as often the elements are stained through mishandling by humans, God cleanses them through the sufferings and pains of those same human creatures'.

Biocide

Biocide is one activity by means of which this generation is irreversibly damaging life for future generations. Nevertheless, this extremely destructive behaviour is ignored by many moralists. Charles Curran, an American moral theologian, overlooks any treatment of biocide in his book *Ongoing Revision in Moral Theology* which was published in 1975.[3] He is not alone. Most discussions of the prohibition of the fifth commandment – 'Thou shalt not Kill' – do the same. Traditional moral treatises concentrated almost exclusively on murder and suicide. In the aftermath of World War II, genocide was added to the list. Today, moralists need to add to their reflection on sin and evil the extinction of species.

In Chapter 2, I discussed in some detail the implications of the extinction of species for human beings, for other members of the Earth community and for the future of the evolutionary process.

A final word on this from J.E. Lovelock: in his book *Gaia*[4] he asks what we would think of an early race of hunters who had developed a taste for horse meat and then proceeded in a short time to hunt the horse to extinction? We would say that they had been lazy, selfish, savage and eminently stupid humans not to have recognized the possibility of a working relationship between humans and the horse. Yet this is exactly what modern man is doing with thousands of living species. Some of the endangered species, such as the sperm whales, have a brain capacity many times larger than that of the human. If we continue to hunt them to extinction we may preclude a co-operative relationship in the area of communication much more spectacular than that existing today between human beings and the horse.

There are two related moral questions that need to be faced here. Under what circumstances is it moral to permit the extinction of any species of animals or plants? When a significant number of species are threatened with extinction, such as twenty percent of the biosphere, with all that implies for every life-form, does that change the moral equation? Do the rights of individual human beings always and forever take precedence over the rights of other species to survive? In the last chapter we saw that the human population has increased considerably over the past century. This is one factor among others which puts pressure on other species and often indirectly involves their extinction. Is there not a serious moral obligation to limit human population levels, especially in countries where thousands of species are on the brink of extinction and the human population is increasing dramatically? There are no simple answers to many of these questions, but given the rate of extinction and what it means for the life of the Earth, moral theologians should grapple with them.

Nuclear Holocaust

The destruction which a nuclear holocaust would bring about also reaches into the future. In fact, it may abort any future. The fear of being vaporized in a nuclear holocaust hangs like a dark cloud over every dawn for many young people today. It almost prevents them from seriously engaging in life. Why undergo the discipline of developing their character and talents if they, and everything they hold dear, can be wiped out in a short time? The horrors of a nuclear war have seized the contemporary imagination through books like Jonathan Schell's *The Fate of the Earth*[5] and television presentations like *The Day After*. The nuclear issue raises very serious questions for religion as it undermines the very foundation of hope in the future. Many older people attempt to banish the sense of impending doom by not thinking about it and adopting a business-as-usual attitude. Others succumb to a crippling despair. They find it difficult to face their despair and work through it in a way that will free them to work with others to lessen the dangers of nuclear war. Admitting to feelings of despair is alien to the whole western religious and moral tradition.

For these and many other reasons, Church leaders have begun to speak out on some of the issues relating to the possession of and use of nuclear weapons. The American bishops, for example, after widespread consultation and two earlier drafts, published an excellent document on the nuclear issue, *The Challenge of Peace*.[6] The document has had a wide impact on people for beyond the boundaries of the Catholic Church both in the United States and elsewhere. A joint statement by the Irish bishops in 1983, called *The Storm That Threatens*, also discusses the issue of war and peace in a nuclear age.[7] It condemns the misuse of scarce resources and human ingenuity involved in creating sophisticated instruments of death when so much needs to be done to support life. The

bishops include a thought-provoking quotation from Pope
John Paul II's speech at the United Nations University in
Hiroshima on 25 February 1981, that 'from now on, it is only
through a deliberate policy that humanity can survive'.

This document recognizes that the threat to life does not
end even with the annihilation of the human species but goes
beyond that. The bishops warn about the possibility of what is
called a nuclear winter. They say that 'nuclear war represents
a potentially catastrophic threat to the physical environment
on which human life depends'.

Recent research has demonstrated that this fear is well
founded. In December 1983, a group of five scientists
published an article in *Science* magazine which claimed that
'the smoke from as few as a thousand fires in a hundred major
cities could cast a sooty pall over the northern hemisphere,
enough to bring darkness at noon and radically cool the
Earth's surface for months, thereby triggering a climatic
catastrophe – a nuclear winter – that would threaten many
plants and animal species, including man, with extinction
(*Sydney Morning Herald*, 25 October 1984).'

Carl Sagan, an astronomer, shares this view. With a group
of other scientists he took part in a two-year study on the
long-term biological consequences of nuclear war. The
conclusions of the study stated that a war involving five
thousand megatons would block out ninety percent of the
sunlight and cause a deep freeze in the northern hemisphere.
The ensuing nuclear winter would so inhibit photosynthesis
that the entire food chain might collapse. One of the findings
of the study came as a surprise. Since both superpowers live in
the northern hemisphere, and in the event of a war, would
target most of their war-heads on each other, the chances of
survival there are minimal. Some experts felt that the southern
hemisphere would be relatively untouched. This study
questioned that assumption. It argued that, because of wind
patterns and ocean currents, the southern hemisphere would
not fare much better. The conclusion emerging from this and
other similar studies should be obvious – any policy of fighting
and winning a nuclear war is the height of lunacy (*The
Guardian Weekly*, 13 November 1983).

The much trumpeted 'strategic defense initiative', the

so-called 'Star Wars' of the Reagan administration, will not do much to allay the above fears. In a speech to the National Catholic Educational Association in St Louis in April 1985, Sagan summed up his opposition to 'Star Wars' in two sentences: 'so if you put all that together – it can be underflown, overwhelmed, it's ruinously expensive, it abrogates solemn treaties and it's likely to precipitate nuclear war – you have quite a package. Except for those problems it is a great idea.'[8]

Numerous episcopal conferences have now spoken out on the dangers of nuclear annihilation. However, few leaders have broadened their vision enough to concede that a constant and increasing rate of destruction to the natural world will have a similar sterilizing effect on the Earth as would the use of nuclear weapons. Probably because of lack of awareness of the true proportions of this challenge, it has not received proper attention from religious leaders. Somewhat ironically, the first important international document to call attention to the moral dimensions of what is happening is the United Nations' *World Charter for Nature*. This document, which was sponsored by Zaire and supported by other Third-World countries, restates the theme of this book clearly and succinctly:[9]

(a) Mankind is a part of nature and life depends on the uninterrupted functioning of natural systems which ensure the supply of energy and nutrients.

(b) Civilization is rooted in nature, which has shaped human culture and influenced all artistic and scientific achievement, and living in harmony with nature gives man the best opportunity for his creativity, and for rest and recreation.

The document then calls for a moral code to guide human interaction with the natural world:

(a) Every form of life is unique, warranting respect regardless of its worth to man, and, to accord other organisms such recognition, man must be *guided by a moral code of action* (italics mine).

(b)   Man can alter nature and exhaust natural resources by his action or its consequence and, therefore, must fully recognize the urgency of maintaining the stability and quality of nature and of conserving natural resources.

The Charter goes on to propose important general principles. The first two are basic. Number one states: 'That nature shall be respected and its essential processes shall not be impaired.' The second principle deals directly with the threat of extinction: 'The genetic viability of the Earth shall not be compromised; the population levels of all life forms, wild and domesticated, must be, at least, sufficient for their survival, and to this end necessary habitats shall be safeguarded.'

Section 2 specifies what measures need to be taken in order to enhance vital ecosystems and to protect those which are most vulnerable and already seriously damaged.

Section 3 deals with the task of implementing the document. Knowledge of natural systems and the principles enshrined in the document shall be disseminated widely at local, national and international levels. It challenges nations, local communities and every individual to be involved in its implementation. The document concludes by insisting that:

Each person has a duty to act in accordance with the provisions of the present Charter; acting individually, in association with others or through participating in the political process, each person shall strive to ensure that the objectives and requirements of the present Charter are met.

Practical Suggestions

This is a prophetic document, calling for extensive changes in the life-style of individuals and whole societies in order to conserve the regenerative capacity of nature. We are thus challenged to be aware of the long-term consequences of our everyday behaviour. We are called to consume less. Peer pressure and continuous advertising have made this genera-tion very acquisitive. We need to wean ourselves away from our excessive urge to amass possessions and learn both to share more and to be happy with less. Many aspects of life should be changed. Clothing should be simple and functional and respond to real needs rather than to passing fashions. We need to change our eating habits, from highly processed foods full of sugar and a high meat diet to food that is home-grown, more healthy and less destructive of the Earth. We should avoid the fast-food restaurants that are destroying the Amazon rain forest. Carrying a shopping basket would save using throwaway plastic containers. Special attention must be paid to conserving scarce fossil fuel. We need to conserve the energy we use both in heating and cooling our houses and for transport. Wherever possible, people should be encouraged to walk or cycle or use public transport.

There are many opportunities for responding to the vision of the World Charter in neighbourhood associations, for example sharing many tools, goods and resources; supporting local consumer co-operatives or local businesses rather than supermarkets or multinational chains, even when the initial cost is higher. The long-term benefits, including utilizing local resources and providing jobs and employment for local people, will strengthen the local community. Both as individuals and as communities people should try to avoid supporting commercial or industrial concerns whose activity is destructive of people and of the Earth.

At Santa Cruz Mission we are trying to implement this vision among the T'boli and the other tribal groups in South Cotabato. The approach of the Mission is never limited to evangelization, narrowly defined. Rather, it attempts to respond in an integrated way to the particular needs of each tribal community. These responses involve opportunities for relevant education, improved health care in each community, better use of land through organic farming and the biological control of pests, the preservation of the tropical rain forest in the province and the conservation of varieties of rice and root crops. The mission also helps develop, expand and market the local crafts and artistic skills of the community. It fosters participation by every age group in the tribes but it is particularly keen that the formal and informal education programmes for young people encourage them to take pride in their music, song, dance, crafts and other facets of their culture. Under the leadership of its present director, Fr Rex Mansmann, the Mission has worked among tribal peoples for over twenty years. Today the fruits of the many years of commitment by the staff members, including priests, sisters and many laypeople, are beginning to show. Because the pressures on tribal peoples have also increased dramatically (as was pointed out in Part 1, Chapter 2) their task of preserving their environment and culture takes on a new urgency.

Politics (as we saw on pages 154–5) must also be transformed by ecological awareness. The *World Charter for Nature* recognizes: 'that competition for scarce resources creates conflicts, whereas the conservation of nature and natural resources contributes to justice and the maintenance of peace and cannot be achieved until mankind learns to live in peace and to forsake war and armaments.'

It is essential to generate a genuine interest among politicians, at both the local and national level, in ecological issues and to support parties and movements that are committed to conservation. The platform of many Green Parties enshrines many of the values I have argued for in this book. They recognize the rootedness of the human in the Earth, the need for decentralization of government decisions and the fact that a sustainable economy must be based on a non-exploitative approach to ecosystems. It is important that everyone, including politicians, recognize that peace will only be achieved when there is justice between peoples and harmony with the Earth.

These are just a few ways in which moral values might challenge us to be conscious of the wider Earth community. Any action which misuses the resources of the Earth, especially if it is destructive of life-forms and does not allow the emergent creative process of the Earth to continue in an integral and effective manner, is intrinsically evil. The reason is simple: it affects this generation and all future generations and life-forms on Earth in a way that involves irreversible damage to life-systems.

Unfortunately, in spite of its comprehensive approach, the *World Charter for Nature* has not received much attention in the media. Religious leaders could take up its challenge, using their moral authority to bring it to people's attention and encourage programmes that implement its recommendations.

12

SPIRITUALITY AND MISSION

The heart of any religious tradition is, of course, its spirituality – the spiritual disciplines which, when taken together, inspire the adherents to live out their lives in accordance with the vision, ideals and norms which the religious tradition embraces. If these spiritual disciplines become lopsided, focused only on selective, peripheral elements within the tradition, or if they distort the truth that must be lived, then the spiritual energies of the faithful are misdirected and can often be quite destructive. Little, however, needs to be said here specifically about spirituality since this entire book emerges from a vision of the world as a bio-spiritual entity. Our vision of the universe, our love for the Earth, our understanding of creation, our worship of God, celebration of the sacraments and moral behaviour are integral to any spirituality. Divorced from this context spirituality is meaningless.

In Part 2, Chapter 6, we discussed how our understanding of reality, including God, is always imperfect and needs to be complemented by the insights of others. Hence any genuine spirituality is essentially communal. In the course of history, spiritually gifted people like St Benedict, St Francis and St Theresa developed distinct spiritualities, appropriate for their time, which continue to enrich the human community today. While these spiritualities are different, each includes the essential Christian beliefs and practices. Our contemporary understanding of the Earth and cosmos as a unique revelation of God could lead to a new authentic spirituality appropriate for our times. The unique, universal elements of this new understanding should enter into, enrich and revitalize all earlier spiritualities.

There is a pressing need to internalize this new more holistic approach to spirituality in order to channel our spiritual energies into creative ventures. Brian Swimme, a scientist who now works at the Institute for Culture and Creation Spirituality in California, has written perceptively:

> When the full story of our origins and our development is comprehended in all its beauty by the human community, the energy released will activate the creativity of the human venture from a depth not hitherto suspected. When we humans realize that our ancestry includes all forms of life, all the stars, the galaxies, even the fireball at the heart of time, when we humans realize that our primary allegiance includes not our nations but also the nations of all species, and the whole stupendous living Earth, then a spring of power will renew the peoples of the planet.[1]

This vision, which includes all reality, is far removed from some of the dualistic strands that we find in our recent spirituality.

There is an anti-body, anti-creatures bias in much of the spiritual literature which was used in houses of religious formation until recently. Some aspects of the early fifteenth-century *Imitation of Christ*, which has for centuries been read by many lay-people and religious, illustrates this tendency. The author, Thomas à Kempis, uses the word 'passion' with a negative connotation, and sums up his approach to nature in a single sentence 'every time I go into creation, I withdraw from God'. Adolfe Tanquerey, an early twentieth-century writer in the same tradition, in his treatise on the spiritual life[2] offers to the novice the prayer of humility: 'May I know Thee, O Lord, that I may love Thee: May I know myself, that I may despise myself.'

Unfortunately this tradition, which divorces spiritual growth from cosmos, the Earth, and the social, political and economic dimensions of human life still lingers within the Church today. Vestiges of it are to be seen in much of the fundamentalist, charismatic religion for whose adherents nothing matters except a personal relationship with Jesus. In the United States, 'electronic preaching' can play on people's guilt, beat the patriotic drum and espouse a muscular, pro-nuclear, pro-capitalist rhetoric which is extremely danger-ous. The charismatic movement in the Catholic Church also tends at times to champion an ahistorical, apolitical approach to religion. There are, of course, notable exceptions. Cardinal Suenens constantly challenges charismatic Christians to bring the dynamism which is so evident at their prayer meetings to bear on the social and economic problems of our times.[3]

A disturbing retreat from the real world is seen today in the proliferation of cults, like the Moonies and Hare Krishna. The cult phenomenon counters the alienation which many people find in the world and the Church today with simplistic solutions to the complex problems of our times. Their rally cry of 'back to the Bible' or 'back to the Koran' overlooks the fact that these sacred books grew out of a particular milieu. While they have much to teach us today, they were not written in response to the specific problems which beset us here and now. Rather than fixating us in the past, these scriptures challenge believers today to respond in as creative a way to the problems of *our* times as Jesus and Mohammed did in theirs. The cults, on the other hand, often encourage their members to withdraw from the real world with its pain and insecurity and to live completely within the walls of the cult's ideology and culture.

Apart from clear-cut answers, the sects also provide an especially powerful experience of companionship and belong-ing which many young people crave for in a highly mechanized, lonely world. The sense of belonging which the cults foster can break down an individual's sense of personal identity. Members may be inclined to surrender their own will and sense of judgement to the will of the guru or leader.

Unfortunately, these cults are not just confined to the fringes of society. They are also found in certain movements within the Catholic Church. These movements are well motivated; they aim to transform the individual, and through the individual, to transform the wider Church and society. However, their understanding of what is involved can be inadequate and they seem to use some methods and tactics employed by the cult movement. If their thinking derives from a Church under threat, fighting back and then victorious, temporally and politically, they will strike anyone in touch with the changing signs of the times as alien.

The spiritual energies of the cults are geared to refashioning the world according to a master plan. However, they generally ignore many of the fundamentally important ecological, economic, social and political problems of our times. When they do this consistently, it is hard to see how they express God's concern for his people as portrayed in the Bible: 'I have seen the misery of my people in Egypt. I have heard their outcry against their slave-masters. I have taken heed of their sufferings, and have come down to rescue them from the power of Egypt, and to bring them up out of the country into a fine, broad land' (Ex. 3:7–8).

Nor do they concur with Jesus's own understanding of his mission which we find in Luke's Gospel, 'The spirit of the Lord is upon me because he has anointed me; he has sent me to announce good news to the poor, to proclaim release for prisoners and recovery of sight for the blind; to let the broken victims go free, to proclaim the year of the Lord's favour' (Luke 4:18–19).

From the experience of liberation theology, during the last twenty years we have also seen the growth of basic Christian communities. This spiritual movement marks a clear break with the dichotomy between the spiritual and the earthly which is characteristic of much that has gone before. It is also much more in keeping with the thrust of the biblical passages quoted above. Finally it arises from the concrete experience of living in situations of gross injustice and oppression and discerning with other members of the Christian community what response this situation should evoke from a follower of Jesus. According to this perspective, given the injustice, oppression and poverty of many people in Latin America and other Third World countries, religious faith is not credible unless it promotes social change, the elimination of injustice and the participation of the poor in decisions that shape their lives. Faith seeks to encounter the Lord of history in the lives of the poor who in the words of the document that came from the Puebla

202 To Care for the Earth

conference, 'are privileged carriers of the Lord, principal heirs of the kingdom, with the potential for evangelizing all nations and the Church as a whole'.[4]

The spirituality that flows from this option for the poor does not lead to a flight from the world, nor does it speak soothing words encouraging the poor to bear with their present sufferings in order to ensure a life of bliss in the next world. Rather it encourages the poor and all who will stand with them to take action to break the chains that shackle them and in the process to free their oppressors as well.

This action and the prayer which sustains it does not take place in isolation but in the midst of a community, where people are actively engaged at all levels in combating injustice. The prayer and action of the Christian community are complementary. Liberation spirituality has touched the lives of bishops, priests, religious and lay people living in small basic communities in Latin America, Southeast Asia and Africa. Within a short space of twenty years; countless Christians involved in action for justice have been martyred. The most notable, to date, is Archbishop Oscar Romero of San Salvador, who was murdered by a right-wing death squad while saying Mass. Others have been tortured and deprived of their freedom.

In 1983 two fellow-Columbans, a Filipino secular priest and six lay Church workers were gaoled in Bacolod on the island of Negros in the Philippines on a trumped-up charge of murdering a local mayor. Their case drew world-wide attention, especially in Ireland and Australia, because there was plenty of documentary evidence to prove that Fr Niall O'Brien was not on the island of Negros when the murder of Mayor Sola took place. The real crime of the priests in the eyes of the military and the sugar planters was that they had worked tirelessly to establish basic Christian communities in the district.

Given the context of poverty and exploitation out of which liberation theology grew, it is understandable that the tools of analysis used by these theologians are mainly sociological and economic, complemented by evaluative tools which are predominantly biblical. Some of the sociological tools are based on certain aspects of Marxist thought. This causes uneasiness, especially among European Church leaders. People involved in sharing liberation theology rebut any exclusive dependence on Marx. Their preferential option for the poor is based on the life and teaching of Jesus.

It is natural that the focus in the early days was on the economic and social conditions of the poor. In my experience here in the Philippines, people who are actively trying to bring about a new social, political and economic order, inspired by the vision of liberation theology, often dismiss ecology as a middle-class concern. They argue that once the human transformation has taken place, then a new, less exploitative, relationship with the natural world will emerge. I have questioned this approach on a number of occasions already in this book. Today it is vital for humans and the Earth that liberation theology begins to include liberation for every species and the Earth itself. Chapter 2 called attention to the fact that the destruction of the tropical forest is one of the largely irreversible evils of our time. There is no place on Earth where the tropical forest is as much under attack as the Amazon basin in South America. Unless the environment is preserved, social justice for all human beings, not to mention other creatures, will simply be a dream.

A number of contemporary spiritual writers are indeed showing a sensitivity to all the Earth, as Fr Basil Pennington O.S.B. shows in the following extract. To bring the marvels of the emergent cosmos and the beauty of the Earth into our prayer and not to be pained by what is happening today would be hypocritical. This new experience of God in the world around us invites us to work for the well-being of all the creatures in the Earth community.

When we realize who God is and who we ourselves are, and the utter gratuity of creation, a total thanksgiving wells up from the very depths of a grateful receiving being. All is gift and gratefully received. Greed is gone. Nothing is taken for granted. All is reverenced: 'I thank you, God, for the wonder of my being.' Ecological well-being is a necessary consequence. There is a loving care for every person and everything. Sufficiency is more than enough, for it is more than is deserved. It is what is wanted for all. And what one has is shared with all, with that end in view.[5]

Ecological prayer must begin with a real experience of God's creation around us, the interrelatedness of all reality, and the divine spark in each reality that can light up our lives. Once again in this area we have so much to learn from tribal people. Older T'boli have a phenomenal knowledge of the plants, insects, birds and animals in their environment and the properties they associate with each. An ecological spirituality is grounded also in the story of the universe. The religious person needs to understand and to be intimate with the natural world in her or his local environment, so that one can feel that in one's prayer one is not just supported by the aspirations and yearnings of the human community but that the Earth community is also participating. This experience of spiritual sustenance from the natural world is very strong in the North American Indian tradition, as can be seen in a book like *Black Elk Speaks*.[6]

A disciplined prayer life is also very important for anyone working to develop an ecological sensitivity in our world. It brings one into contact with the self-giving love of the One who is the ground of all Being. God's fatherly and motherly love is poured out into all the creatures of the Earth. An intimate experience of this centre of all reality is a necessary antidote to the despair that so much of the data presented seems to evoke. In prayer the religious person experiences a God who is faithful to his promises.

Celtic Spirituality

A spirituality for our modern age cannot be built exclusively on the insights, prayers, rituals, myths, symbols and devotional practices of former ages. The theme of this book is that an authentic spirituality must emerge from our understanding of the Earth today and an awareness of the challenge of our times. While this is true, a genuine spirituality also draws upon tradition. If we re-examine the past, we often discover insights and practices of our ancestors, believers or not, whose deepest meaning they themselves did not fully comprehend. For example, traditional Celtic spirituality which emerged from the marriage of the Christian tradition and the pre-Christian traditional religion was particularly sensitive to the presence of God in the natural world, and so it has much to teach Irish men and women today. The Scottish Episcopalian theologian John Macquarrie calls attention to this aspect of Celtic spirituality in his book *Paths in Spirituality.*[7]

> Although it [Celtic spirituality] belongs to a culture that has almost vanished it fulfils in many aspects the condition to which a contemporary spirituality would have to conform. At the very centre of this type of spirituality was an intense sense of presence. The Celt was very much a God-intoxicated man whose life was embraced on all sides by the Divine Being. *But this presence was always mediated through some finite, this-world reality, so that it would be difficult to imagine a spirituality more down to earth than this one.* The sense of God's immanence in his creation was so strong in Celtic spirituality as to amount sometimes almost to pantheism. (Italics mine.)

In pre-Christian Celtic religion, powerful spirits were associated with the forces of nature. The ancient Celts recognized water as the first principle and source of life. Many of the major rivers of Western Europe still have Celtic names – the Rhine, the Marne, the Seine, the Clyde and the Severn. The sources of these rivers inspired a particular veneration as can be seen from archaeological remains all over what was once Celtic Europe. These rivers were associated with an array of Celtic fertility goddesses. Sacred wells, like the great healing centre in Bath in Britain, and local springs were placed under the protection of the Mother goddess. All through the Christian era, and to this day in many parts of Ireland, holy wells continue to play an important role in the popular devotion of the people.

Trees and sacred groves were also seen as abodes of the spirits. In the transition to Christianity, monastic churches, like that of St Columcille in Derry, were built in a clearing within a sacred grove. In a nature poem of the eighteenth or nineteenth century, the monk is portrayed as being at home in

the company of creatures. He is familiar with their habitat and
knows their ways. Living without other human beings in the
wood is for him a rich community experience. There is no
hankering for human companions. He feels at one and at peace
with the world around him and with God.[8]

MARBAN, A HERMIT SPEAKS

For I inhabit a wood
    unknown but to my God
my house of hazel and ash
    as an old hut in a rath.

And my house small, not too small,
    is always accessible:
women disguised as blackbirds
    talk their words from its gable.

The stags erupt from rivers,
    brown mountains tell the distance:
I am glad as poor as this
    even in men's absence.

Death-green of yew,
huge green of oak
sanctify,
and apples grow
close by new nuts:
water hides.

Young of all things,
bring faith to me,
guard my door:
the rough, unloved
wild dogs, tall deer,
quiet does.

In small tame bands
the badgers are,
grey outside:
and foxes dance
before my door
all the night.

all at evening
the day's first meal
     since dawn's bread:
trapped trout, sweet sloes
and honey, haws,
     beer and herbs.

Moans, movements of
silver-breasted
birds rouse me:
pigeons perhaps.
And a thrush sings
constantly.

Black-winged beetles
boom, and small bees;
     November
through the lone geese
a wild winter
     music stirs.

Come fine white gulls
all sea-singing
and less sad,
lost in heather,
the grouse's song,
little sad.

For music I
have pines, my tall
     music-pines
so who can I
envy here, my
     gentle Christ?

The monk feels nurtured and protected by nature. Early
Irish poetry has a lively appreciation for beauty and nature.
Descriptions of nature are fresh, vivid and speak of a close
bond between the poet and his surroundings. This is clearly
evident in the following ninth-century poem.[9]

I have news for you: The stag bells, winter snows,
summer has gone.

Wind high and cold, the sun low, short its course, the sea running high,
Deep red the bracken its shape is lost; wild goose has raised its customed cry.
Cold has seized the bird's wing; season of ice, this is my news.

While a love of nature is very evident among the early Celts and great store is placed on the fertility of land and flocks, it would not be accurate to present them as models of ecological rectitude in modern terms. The *Fiannaiocht* literature certainly contains moving descriptions of the beauty of nature. At the same time there is high praise for the joys of hunting, and a good 'kill' greatly enhanced a warrior's reputation. In common with most ancient peoples the Celts felt that the environment was fairly permanent. Given their technology it took many generations to change the environment substantially – changes which today we can bring about in a short period because of our vastly more powerful technology. The human pressure on the environment was not heavy. In ancient times there were probably less than 100,000 people living in Ireland. At that time the interior of the country was covered with marshes, bogs and impassable forests, so it was natural that the *Fiannaiocht* literature would celebrate the achievements of the heroes who cut down the forest, drained the swamps and opened up the land for pasture.

The traditional Celtic sensitivity for the presence of the Divine in the world of nature is also found in Joseph Mary Plunkett's poem *I See His Blood Upon the Rose*, written in the early part of this century.[10]

I see his blood upon the rose
And in the stars the glory of his eyes,
His body gleams amid eternal snows,
His tears fall from the skies.

I see his face in every flower;
The thunder and singing of the birds
Are but his voice – and carven by his power;
Rocks are his written words.

All pathways by his feet are worn,
His strong heart stirs the ever-beating sea,
His crown of thorns is twined with every thorn,
His cross is every tree.

Within the context of the cosmic christology outlined on pages 118-119, this poem directs our attention to Christ's presence in the stars, the flowers, the thunder in the sky and the song of the birds.

The Celtic spiritual heritage, like any other, is not something to be copied in detail, irrespective of its appropriateness for our times. The Irish Forest and Wildlife Service would not be impressed if modern Irish poets extolled the virtues of those who cut down the forest and destroy wildlife! Even so, there is much that we can learn from the early poets' reverence for the presence of God in the natural world which can guide and sustain us in our search for an ecologically sound ethic and spirituality. This vision could once again call forth the heroic spirit of the Celtic monks so famous for the arduous journeys they undertook in order to preach the message of Christ in Europe.

Mission

The mention of mission brings me back to what I wrote at the beginning of this book. The ideas presented here have emerged from my missionary experience in the Philippines. So I think it is important to sketch some implications of the positions espoused here for mission in the world today.

It would be a gross over-simplification to present the missionary enterprise of any era as a homogeneous operation. For one thing, missionaries were often working in continents thousands of miles apart, with little opportunity to communicate among themselves. What's more, the vast cultural differences among those who were being evangelized, and the fact that many missionaries were strong and determined people, made any rigid approach impossible.

Having said this, it is true that major common themes, ideals and values did characterize the missionary thrust of different ages and missionaries were caught up in the fever of their times. Spanish and Portuguese missionaries followed closely in the footsteps of the great explorers, Vasco de Gama, Columbus and Magellan. They accompanied the conquistadores – Cortes in Latin America and Legaspi in the Philippines.

In one way or another, the missionaries were involved in the great movements and yearnings of their times. The vision, energy, courage and perseverence needed to sustain the missionary movement was truly enormous. This is evident, for example, in Fr Martin Noone's book *The Islands Saw It*,[11] where he describes the arrival of the Spanish in the Philippines and the early years of Spanish settlement.

While the Spanish and Portuguese missionaries were intimately involved in the colonial process, the secular and religious elements were not always hand-in-glove. Some missionaries – too few from our point in history – were extremely critical of the colonial civil and military administration. Bartolomé de las Casas is remembered today in Latin America for his vigorous defence of indigenous people in the Caribbean and in South America. The first bishop of Manila, Domingo de Salazar, played a somewhat similar role in the Philippines. Many lesser known missionaries, who were in general in agreement with the colonial drive, nevertheless mitigated the brutality of the colonizers by preaching the humanity of the Gospel.

In the nineteenth century, Catholic and Protestant missionaries also accompanied the new colonial powers – Britain, France and Germany – to the farthest limits of Africa, Oceania and Asia. Once again, like their secular counterparts working in the civil service or the army, many were intoxicated by the vision of the age. They concentrated on the bright side of the colonial venture – that schools and health care were bringing enlightment to those who lived in darkness. With some notable exceptions, missionaries were inclined to overlook the fact that the colonial expansion in the nineteenth century had a brutal and very destructive impact on non-western societies. In India, for example, the colonial administration destroyed a thriving textile industry because it was in competition with the mills in England. The social, economic and political policies were framed in such a way as to keep the indigenous people always in a subservient position. This reflected attitudes that now seem racist and paternalistic.

Missionaries shared most of the attitudes of other colonials. Many showed little respect for indigenous cultures and set about Europeanizing their converts as if that was absolutely necessary in order to Christianize them. Yet, despite the excesses of the colonial powers, many missionaries worked tirelessly to set up an impressive network of schools, clinics, hospitals, and orphanages to serve the people among whom they worked. In the area of ethnographic research, some of the best accounts of tribal cultures in the eighteenth and nineteenth centuries were written by sympathetic missionaries.

We might ask, what are the great yearnings of our own time to which missionaries might respond with the energy and enthusiasm that inspired missionaries of earlier ages? In December 1981, SEDOS brought together experts from around the world to reflect on the meaning of mission today and to plan for the future. The proceedings of the seminar were later published by Orbis Press as *Mission in Dialogue*.[12]

The seminar grouped the present trends in mission work under four headings: Proclamation, Inculturation, Liberation and Dialogue. That dialogue is the hallmark of missionary praxis today is clear from the title. Inculturation, liberation and dialogue between faiths certainly respond to the deepest yearnings of people around the world today. The search for authentic cultural identity among peoples is widespread.

Care for the Earth is one of the major concerns of our times which is missing from the list. I feel that the acceptance of the *World Charter for Nature* by the United Nations is a significant milestone in human–Earth relations. It is a sign that the United Nations has come of age and an indication that the ecological movement is growing both at the grass roots and among some political leaders.

Few missionaries, either as individuals or as members of missionary congregations or institutions, have caught up with this world-wide aspiration and explored its missionary dimensions. *Mission in Dialogue* has only a few references to pollution, particularly in Japan. Not a single contributor saw either the scale or the seriousness of the problem. Even when they spoke about social justice they did not see the need to extend their vision of justice to the total Earth community. Although this oversight is regrettable, it hardly comes as a surprise seeing that environmental concerns have, as yet, made little impact on religious people. Recent efforts within the Society of St Columban provide a good indicator of contemporary missionary concerns and objectives. Article 11 of the first draft of the constitutions combined a statement on ecology with a statement on social justice and presented both as central to evangelization today.

> We are concerned with the totality of life. The Spirit leads us to a deep respect for the beauty of the world and the balance in nature. He also leads us to a deep appreciation for the dignity and excellence of people. Violence to the ecological balance in nature and violence to the rights of people, are a contradiction of the Gospel. This is a central concern in our lives. The Spirit that guides us makes us co-creators and co-redeemers with Jesus, the Lord of History.

The second, third and fourth drafts, reflecting negative or, at least, indifferent feedback from a wide segment of opinion among the members, dropped the above article. Concern for the environment remains a somewhat esoteric pursuit. Individual missionaries may well support environmental action groups, but this is not seen as central to the missionary vocation in precisely the way the drafters of the article had in mind. One hopes that the situation will change rapidly in the next few years and that care for the Earth will no longer be peripheral to missionary activity. Missionaries are in a unique position to bring the message of caring for the Earth to the wider Church and society. I have argued on page 2 that missionaries bring together the experience of people in both the Third- and First-Worlds. Today, the thrust of many individual missionaries and institutes is to build across the globe networks geared to work for justice. In my discussion on liberation theology I argued that these groups need to widen their vision even further to include a concern for the Earth.

Missionaries also are people who live in two cultures. Here again they span two articulations of the human experience. They are born, reared and educated in one culture and they minister in another. If their experience of mission has been in any way profound it helps them to revitalize their own cultural experience. They often learn to appreciate its strengths and also its weaknesses, and to be enriched by the insights of the people among whom they minister. One of the central points of this book is that the western consumer culture is damaging the fabric of the Earth. Those living in First-World countries who have never known anything else cannot conceive how life might be organized in a different way. Here the experience of missionaries working in cultures that live lightly on the Earth is invaluable.

This new emphasis is in continuity with some of the best missionary traditions of the past. Even in the Philippines the Spanish missionaries never confined themselves to preaching the Gospel, narrowly defined, or to celebrating the sacraments and doing works of mercy. The coming of Christianity had a profound impact on many aspects of Philippine life and culture despite the lack of sensitivity that most missionaries displayed towards indigenous religious values. Nick Joaquin, a Filipino novelist, lists some of these:

> Christianity in the Philippines is wheel and plough, is road and bridge, is irrigation dam and canal, is grain in the field and fruit on the tree and vegetable in the garden, is the Pangasinan oxen and Batangas beef and the horses at the Rancerias, is tobacco factory and sugar refinery, is calendar and clock and recorded history and our sense of Faustian time, is the cuisine that makes us a people and the map that makes us a nation, is the trade that's every town's fiesta and the ancient tower that continues to gather us under the sound of the bell.[13]

What a tribute to the missionaries of our time if a future historian could say that the missionary movement of the latter part of the twentieth century encouraged all Christians and religious people everywhere to care for the Earth! If it meant clean air, fertile lands farmed to produce an array of nutritious crops, unpolluted seas and rivers teeming with fish, vast forest areas protected against intruders, and vibrant, mainly self-sufficient, human communities living in harmony with each other and with nature, celebrating in wonder the bountifulness of the Earth and protecting its fruitfulness for future generations! This vision certainly is idealistic given the present disparities between peoples and the rate of destruction of the Earth. Nevertheless, it is based on the insight of the prophets of the Old Testament, the deepest aspirations of the religions of the Earth, the teachings of Jesus and the wisdom of our own age as told in the story of the universe. It could inspire a new generation of missionaries and Christians enthusiastically to dedicate their lives to making this vision a reality. As always the need is great, probably greater today than ever before because this generation faces ultimate challenges. We hear the challenge of Moses in Deuteronomy 30:19–20 in a new and frightening way: 'I offer you the choice of life or death, blessing or curse. Choose life and then you and your descendants will live.'

If this generation does not choose life, then the story of the twenty billion years of the emergence of the universe will be frustrated in its deepest and more splendid manifestations on planet Earth. If it does choose life, then human beings will enhance the whole emergent process so that we can move into a new and more fruitful bio-spiritual era. In this way the Gospel will be good news for the life of the world.

The previous line sums up the central concerns of this book – good news and life. In the T'boli hills I have watched many of the conditions for abundant life being systematically destroyed. If this destruction continues it could mean the extinction of the T'boli culture. The same forces which are destroying the T'boli world, though not always as evident, are also at work in the United States, Ireland and Australia – countries in which I have studied and taught. Unfortunately, religious people and especially religious leaders do not appear to be aware of what is happening. Very little reflection on this damaging relationship between human beings and the Earth has emerged from Christian thinkers. This book is a modest contribution in that direction. It raises serious and complex questions which the human community must wrestle with now. It also provides some pointers for a new era wherein people will begin actively to care for the Earth.

BIBLIOGRAPHY

Part 1

Chapter 1

1. *Evangelii Nuntiandi*, 1975. St Paul's Publications, Manila.
2. *Inaestimabile Donum*, 1980. Sacred Congregation for Sacraments and Divine Worship. Vatican City.
3. *Instruction on Certain Aspects of the Theology of Liberation*, 1984. Sacred Congregation for Doctrine and Faith. Vatican City.
4. *Populorum Progressio*, 1967. St Paul's Publications, Manila.
5. *Apostolic Letter to Cardinal Roy*, 1971. St Paul's Publications, Manila.
6. *Justice in the World*, 1971. Synod of Bishops. St Paul's Publications, Manila.
7. McCoy, Alfred, 1984. *Priests on Trial*. Sydney, Penguin Books.
8. *Apostolic Letter to Cardinal Roy*, No. 21. *Op. cit.*
9. *L'Osservatore Romano*, Weekly edition, 26 August 1985. pp. 7–8.
10. Berry, Thomas. *Newsletter of the Center for Reflection on the Second Law*. 8420 Camellia Drive, Raleigh, North Carolina. Circular No. 53.

Chapter 2

1. Odum, E., 1971. *Fundamentals of Ecology*. W.B. Saunders Company, Philadelphia, p. 3.
2. Commoner, B., 1972. *The Closing Circle*. New Bantam Books, New York, pp. 29–44.
3. *Multinational Monitor*, August 1984. Washington, D.C. 20036.
4. *Profits From Poison*. Farmers Assistance Board, Inc., P.O. Box AC–623, Quezon City, Philippines.
5. *Global 2000 Report to the President*, 1982. A report prepared by the Council on Environmental Quality and the Department of Energy.

215

6. *Gaia: An Atlas of Planet Management*, 1984. General editor, Dr Norman Myers. Anchor Books, New York.
7. 'Mindanao Wood Industry', in *Showcases of Underdevelopment*, Alternate Resource Center, Davao City, Philippines.
8. Berry, Thomas, *Riverdale Papers* Vol. 8. Riverdale Center for Religious Studies, Riverdale, New York 10471. (unpublished)
9. Caufield, Catherine. 'A Reporter at Large', *New Yorker*, 14 January 1985, pp. 47–99.
10. Berry, Thomas. *Riverdale Papers* Vol. 8. *Op.cit.*
11. Quoted by Matthew Fox in *Cry of the Environment*, 1984. Bear and Company, Inc., P.O. Drawer 2860, Santa Fe, NM 87504, p. 90.
12. Sancti Thomae Aquinatis, *Summa Theologiae*, Biblioteca De Autores Christianos, MCMLVI.

Chapter 3

1. *The State of the Environment*, 1985. An Foras Forbartha, Dublin, Editor, David Cabot.
2. Elsdon, R., 1980. *Bent World*. Inter-Varsity Press, Leicester LE1 7GP, England, p. 40.
3. *The State of the Environment. Op.cit.*, p. 52.
4. *Ibid.* 84.
5. Blackwell, John and Convery, Frank, 1983. *Promise and Performance: Irish Environmental Problems Analysed*. The Resources and Environmental Policy Centre, UCD, Dublin, p. 409.
6. Blackwell, John, 1981. *Environmental Problems in Ireland: A Report to the Churches*.

Chapter 4

1. Berry, Thomas. *The New Story*, Teilhard Studies No. 1, Winter 1978. American Teilhard Association for the Future of Man, 86 Madison Ave., New York, N.Y. 10021.
2. Ziegler, P., 1969. *The Black Death*. Harper Torchbooks, New York, pp. 259–279.
3. Quoted in Mason, Stephen F., 1962. *A History of the Sciences*, Collier Books, New York, p. 27.
4. *Ibid.*, p. 255.
5. *Ibid.*, p. 168.
6. Noble, D., 1977. *America by Design: Science, Technology and the Rise of Corporate Capitalism*. Oxford University Press, pp. 179ff.
7. *Laborem Exercens*, 1981. Pope John Paul II. St Paul's Publications, Manila.
8. Berry, Wendell, 1981. *The Gift of Good Land*. North Point Press, San Francisco, p. 113.

Chapter 5

1. Eliade, M., 1976. *Occultism, Witchcraft and Cultural Fashions. Essays in Comparative Religion*, University of Chicago Press, p. 12.
2. Huxley, J. Introduction to Teilhard de Chardin, *The Phenomenon of Man*. Fontana Books, p. 21.
3. *Phenomenon of Man*, p. 329.
4. *Ibid.*, p. 244.
5. *Ibid.*, p. 243.
6. Lovelock, J.E., 1979. *Gaia: A New Look at Life on Earth*. Oxford University Press.
7. *The New Story, Op.cit.*
8. Teilhard de Chardin, P., *The Phenomenon of Man, Op.cit.*, p. 30.
9. Carson, Rachel, 1962. *Silent Spring*, Fawcett Crest. New York.
10. McCoy, Alfred, 1984. *Priests on Trial, Op.cit.*
11. Casiño, Eric. 'Two Kingdoms', in *Filipino Heritage*, 1977 Vol. 4, pp. 738–41, Lahing Pilipino Publishing Inc., Manila.
12. Schumacher, E.F., 1973. *Small is Beautiful*, Perennial Library, Harper and Row, New York. p. 136.

Part 2

Chapter 6

1. Bird, Phyllis, 1983. *Images of Women in the Old Testament*, ed. Gottwald, Norman, pp. 252–89. Orbis Books, New York.
2. Turner, Frederick, 1980. *Beyond Geography: The Western Spirit Against the Wilderness*, Viking Press, New York.
3. Congar, Yves. 'The Spirit as God's Femininity'. *Theology Digest*, Summer 1982, pp. 129–32.
4. Thomas Berry personal communication.
5. Peters, Ted F., in *Cry of the Environment, Op.cit.*, pp. 415–16.
6. Anderson, Bernhard W., 'Creation and the Noachic Covenant' pp. 45–62 in *Cry of the Environment*.
7. *Ibid.*, pp. 47–51.
8. Berry, Wendell, *Op.cit.*
9. Brunner, Emil, 1952. *Dogmatics*, Vol. 2, *The Christian Doctrine of Creation and Redemption*, Lutterworth, England.
10. Lyonnet, Stanislas, 1965. *Redemption of the Universe*, p. 432, in Contemporary New Testament Studies, The Liturgical Press, Collegeville, Minnesota.
11. *Ibid.*, pp. 423–36.

Chapter 7

1. Dubos, R., 1980. *Wooing the Earth*, Charles Scribner's Sons, New York.
2. Berry, Wendell. *The Gift of Good Land, Op.cit.* p. 281.

3. St Francis of Assisi. *The Canticle of Brother Sun, Omnibus Source*, pp. 130–1, Franciscan Herald Press, Illinois 60609.
4. Hildegarde of Bingen, *Meditations with Hildegarde of Bingen*, translated by Uhlein, Gabriele, 1982, p. 56. Bear and Company, P.O. Santa Fe, NM 87504–2860.
5. *Ibid.*, p. 65.
6. *Ibid.*, p. 51.
7. White, L., 1967. 'Historical Roots of our Ecological Crisis', *Science* pp. 1203–7.
8. Dubos, R., 1972. *A God Within*, New York, Charles Scribner's Sons.
9. Nisbet, R., 1980. *The History of the Idea of Progress*, New York, Basic Books, p. 352.

Chapter 8

1. Radhakrishna Rao, B., 'The Concept of Ecology in Vedic Literature', in *Mazingira*, No. 4, 1982, pp. 68–80, 70.
2. *Ibid.*, 71.
3. *Ibid.*, 75.
4. Berry, Thomas, 1975. *Buddhism*, Thomas Crowell, New York, pp. 40–1.
5. Wang Yang-ming, 'Industry on the Great Learning', in Ecological Prayer, Doland St John, *Encounter*, Autumn 1982, p. 343.
6. 'The Western Inscription', *Introduction to Oriental Civilization*, Sources of Chinese Tradition, ed. Theodore Du Berry, p. 524, Columbia Press, New York.
7. Thomas, Keith, 1983. *Man and the Natural World*, Pantheon Books, New York. p. 35.
8. 'The Western Inscription', *Op.cit.*
9. Chief Seattle, quoted from *Action for World Development Victorian Newsletter*, June 1984, Melbourne.
10. Deloria, Vine Jr, 1973. *God is Red*. A Laurel Book, Dell Publishing Co., Inc., New York.
11. Ninomiya Sontoku, *Nihou Shisoshi Taikei*, Vol. 52, Iwanami Bookstore 1977. Translated by Sr Yasuko Shimezii.

Chapter 9

1. Schumacher, E.F., *Small is Beautiful*, Harper and Row, New York.
2. Capra, Fritjof and Spretnak, Charlene, 1986. *Green Politics: Global Promise*, Bear & Company, Santa Fe.
3. Berry, Thomas, Riverdale Papers Vol. 7: *American College in the Ecological Age.* (unpublished)
4. Illich, Ivan, 1971. *Celebrations of Awareness; A Call For Institutional Revolution*, Anchor Books, New York.

5. Freire, Paulo, 1971. *Pedagogy of the Oppressed*, Herder and Herder, New York.
6. Berry, Thomas. *Op.cit.*
7. Douglas, Mary, 1972. *Natural Symbols*. Penguin, London.
   Geertz, Clifford, 1973. *The Interpretation of Cultures*, Basic Books, New York.
   Ricoeur, P., 1969. *The Symbolism of Evil*, Beacon Press, Boston.
   Turner, Victor, 1969. *The Ritual Process, Structure and Anti-Structure*, Aldine, New York.

Chapter 10

1. Powledge, Fred, 1982. *Water, The Nature, Uses and Future of Our Most Precious and Abused Resource*, Farrar Straus Giroux, New York.
2. Arrupe, Pedro, 1976. *Hunger For Bread and Evangelization*, Sedos, March 1983, Via Dei Verbiti 1, 00154 Rome.
3. Lappe, F.M. and McCallie, E. in *Bread and Justice* by McGinnis, James, Paulist Press, New York, p. 99.
4. Fox, Matthew, 1983. *Original Blessing*, p. 113, Bear and Company, Santa Fe, NM 87504–2860.
5. *Gaudium et Spes*. No. 80 *Vatican Council II*, Liturgical Press, Collegeville, MN 56321.
6. *Lineamenta*, 1982. Reconciliation and Peace in the Church, Vatican City.
7. *Reconciliatio et Paenitentia* 1984, John Paul II, St Paul's Publications.
8. Hildegarde, *Op.cit.*
9. 'Pro Mundi Vita', *Megalopolis*, Bulletin 99, No. 4, 1980, 6 Rue de la Limite 6, B 1030 Brussels.
10. Laing, John E., *Metro Manila Times*, Tuesday, 28 May 1985.

Chapter 11

1. Haring, Bernard, 1982. *Free and Faithful in Christ*, pp. 167–202, St Paul's Publications, Slough.
2. Fox, Matthew, 1983. *Original Blessing*, Bear and Company, Santa Fe, New Mexico, p. 59.
3. Curran, Charles, 1975. *Ongoing Revision in Moral Theology*, Claretian, Notre Dame, Indiana 46556.
4. Lovelock, J.E., 1979. *Gaia: A New Look at Life on Earth*, Oxford University Press, p. 150.
5. Schell, J., 1982. *The Fate of the Earth*, Avon Books, New York.
6. *The Challenge of Peace* 1983, Pastoral letter of the Bishops of the United States.
7. *The Storm that Threatens*. Joint Pastoral letter of the Bishops of Ireland on war and peace in the nuclear age.

8. Speech to the National Catholic Educational Association in St Louis, April 1985.
9. United Nations, *World Charter for Nature*.

Chapter 12

1. Swimme, Brian, 'The Scientist: A Personal Story', work in progress.
2. Tanquerey, A., quoted in Matthew Fox, *Original Blessing*, p. 59.
3. Some of these themes are discussed in a book by Cardinal Suenens and Dom Helder Camara called *Charismatic Renewal and Social Action: A Dialogue* (1984, Claretian Publications, Quezon City, Philippines). While I was writing this book a very insightful book *Spirituality and Justice*, by Donal Dorr (1985, Claretian Publications, Quezon City, Philippines) came to my attention. Dorr avoids or explains in fairly simple terms much of the jargon which tend to frighten people away from any in-depth understanding of the structures at work in any given society. The author shows a thorough understanding of the political, economic, social and ecclesiastical problems which bedevil both First- and Third-World countries. One of the most attractive features of the book for someone like myself who is working in the field is the personal style of the author. It is obvious to me that he has wrestled with these questions in the presence of the Lord. The book attempts – I feel successfully – to build a bridge between the prayer experience of charismatic Christians and the call that all Christians should feel today to be actively involved in building up the Kingdom of God. Unfortunately many contemporary religious movements are moving in the opposite direction.
4. *Puebla and Beyond* 1979. Orbis Books, New York, No. 1147.
5. Pennington, Basil, 'Prayer and Liberation' in *America*, 9 May 1981, pp. 378–80.
6. *Black Elk Speaks, Being the Life Story of a Holy Man of the Oglala Sioux*, told by John G. Neihardt, 1972, Pocket Books, New York.
7. Macquarrie, John, 1983. 'Paths in Spirituality' in *Irish Spirituality*, ed. Maher, Michael, Veritas, Dublin, p. 7.
8. Montague, John (ed.), 1974. *The Faber Book of Irish Verse*, Faber and Faber, London, pp. 57–8.
9. Sharkey, John, 1975. *Celtic Mysteries. The Ancient Religion*, Avon Publications, New York, p. 14.
10. Plunkett, Joseph Mary, 1934, in *Prose and Poetry of England*, ed. H. Ward McGraw, The Singer Company, Chicago.
11. Noone, Martin, 1982. *The Islands Saw It. The Discovery and Conquest of the Philippines. 1521–1581*, Helicon Press, Dublin.
12. Motte, Mary and Lang, Joseph, 1982. *Mission in Dialogue*, Orbis Press, New York.
13. Joaquin, Nick, 'Technology and Philippine Revolutions: The Coming of the Plough, the Horse and Guisado', *The Filipinas Journal*, Vol. 3, 1982, p. 127.

INDEX

221